GW00597914

The Global Economic System

The Global Economic System

HOW LIQUIDITY SHOCKS AFFECT FINANCIAL INSTITUTIONS AND LEAD TO ECONOMIC CRISES

GEORGE CHACKO, CAROLYN L. EVANS,
HANS GUNAWAN, ANDERS SJÖMAN

Vice President, Publisher: Tim Moore
Associate Publisher and Director of Marketing: Amy Neidlinger
Executive Editor: Jim Boyd
Editorial Assistant: Pamela Boland
Senior Marketing Manager: Julie Phifer
Assistant Marketing Manager: Megan Colvin
Cover Designer: Alan Clements
Managing Editor: Kristy Hart
Project Editor: Betsy Harris
Copy Editor: Geneil Breeze
Proofreader: Williams Woods Publishing
Indexer: Lisa Stumpf
Senior Compositor: Gloria Schurick
Manufacturing Buyer: Dan Uhrig

© 2011 by Pearson Education, Inc.
Publishing as FT Press
Upper Saddle River, New Jersey 07458

**This book is sold with the understanding that neither the author nor the publisher is
engaged in rendering legal, accounting, or other professional services or advice by
publishing this book. Each individual situation is unique. Thus, if legal or financial advice
or other expert assistance is required in a specific situation, the services of a competent
professional should be sought to ensure that the situation has been evaluated carefully
and appropriately. The author and the publisher disclaim any liability, loss, or risk resulting directly or indirectly, from the use or application of any of the contents of this book.**

FT Press offers excellent discounts on this book when ordered in quantity for bulk purchases or
special sales. For more information, please contact U.S. Corporate and Government Sales,
1-800-382-3419, corpsales@pearsontechgroup.com. For sales outside the U.S., please contact
International Sales at international@pearson.com.

Company and product names mentioned herein are the trademarks or registered trademarks of
their respective owners.

All rights reserved. No part of this book may be reproduced, in any form or by any means, without
permission in writing from the publisher.

Printed in the United States of America

First Printing June 2011

ISBN-10: 0-13-705012-7
ISBN-13: 978-0-13-705012-3

Pearson Education LTD.
Pearson Education Australia PTY, Limited.
Pearson Education Singapore, Pte. Ltd.
Pearson Education North Asia, Ltd.
Pearson Education Canada, Ltd.
Pearson Educación de Mexico, S.A. de C.V.
Pearson Education—Japan
Pearson Education Malaysia, Pte. Ltd.

Library of Congress Cataloging-in-Publication Data

The global economic system : how liquidity shocks affect financial institutions and lead to economic
crises / George Chacko ... [et al.].

    p. cm.

  ISBN 978-0-13-705012-3 (hbk. : alk. paper)

  1. International finance. 2. Liquidity (Economics) 3. Financial crises. I. Chacko, George.

  HG3881.G57534 2011

  332'.042—dc22

2011010482

George dedicates this to Hemu, Manju, Leah, and Shreya.

Carolyn thanks her father and mother for all their support.

Hans dedicates this book to his loving parents.

Anders is, as always, in constant awe of Alvar.

Contents

Acknowledgments

George Chacko and Carolyn Evans would like to gratefully acknowledge financial support from the Leavey School of Business at Santa Clara University.

About the Authors

George Chacko is Associate Professor of Finance at Santa Clara University's Leavey School of Business and formerly Associate Professor at Harvard Business School, Managing Director at State Street Bank, and Chief Investment Officer at Auda Alternative Investments. He holds a Ph.D. and M.A. in Business Economics from Harvard University and a B.S. from MIT.

Carolyn L. Evans is Associate Professor of Economics at Santa Clara University. She has worked at the Federal Reserve Bank of New York, the Federal Reserve Board of Governors, and the White House Council of Economic Advisers. She holds a Ph.D. and M.A. in Economics and a B.A. in East Asian Languages and Civilizations, all from Harvard University.

Hans Gunawan is Senior Financial Analyst at Skyline Solar and formerly a manager of financial planning and analysis at JAPFA. He holds an MBA from Santa Clara University and a B.S. from University of California, Berkeley.

Anders Sjöman is Vice President of Communications at Voddler. He was formerly Senior Researcher for Harvard Business School's Paris-based Europe Research Center. He holds an M.Sc. from the Stockholm School of Economics.

chapter 1

Motivation for Understanding Liquidity Risk

The global economic crisis of 2008 and 2009 caught many of the most astute investors in the financial markets by surprise. While only 49 hedge funds failed during all of 2007, 344 hedge funds failed during just the third quarter of 2008, and another 778 hedge funds failed during the fourth quarter of 2008. Similarly, while only 3 banks failed in 2007, 25 banks failed in 2008, and 140 failed in 2009. Endowment funds, the financial backbone of private universities, which had posted stellar investment results throughout the 2000s, had an investment return of -19% during fiscal 2009. The four biggest funds, with widely acclaimed investment managers, posted returns of -27% (Harvard), -25% (Yale), -27% (Stanford), and -23% (Princeton). Private equity funds lost 15% in 2008.

As a description of the money management industry during 2008-2009, one of the most widely circulated quotes was provided by the "sage of Omaha," Warren Buffet, who once said "you only find out who is swimming naked when the tide goes out."[1] So how did some of the smartest investors, who had generated outsized returns for a long time with their skills, get caught flat-footed by the largest financial crisis the world had seen in several decades? Were they all in reality "swimming naked"?

1.1 Peso Problem

In his famous quote, Buffet is referring to a phenomenon known in academic circles as a "peso problem"—a term commonly attributed to Nobel laureate Milton Friedman for comments he made about trading in the Mexican peso in the early 1970s. At the time, the exchange rate between the U.S. dollar and the Mexican peso was fixed at that time as both countries were following the Bretton Woods Agreements. However, looking at interest rates on government bonds in Mexico and comparing them to interest rates on similar-maturity government bonds in the United States, one found that the interest rates in Mexico were far higher—despite the fixed exchange rate. This posed a bit of a puzzle. Investors could borrow U.S. dollars and pay a low interest rate, convert these dollars into pesos, and then invest the pesos into Mexican government bonds and earn a high interest rate. When the Mexican bonds matured, the investor could simply convert the peso principal and interest back into dollars at the same exchange rate that he did the initial conversion. He could then pay back the dollar borrowings and he would be left with a profit, equal to the interest rate differential between Mexican and U.S. interest rates times the principal amount borrowed. In modern terms, this is known as a *carry trade*. However because the exchange rate was fixed, there was no risk in this carry trade. Therefore the profit from the carry trade could be earned with no risk—a condition that financial economists refer to as an *arbitrage*, or free money. How could this prevail in the financial markets? In trying to explain this phenomenon, Friedman noted that perhaps the interest rate differential between the two countries reflected a hidden risk factor that no one could observe in financial market data because the downside effects of this risk had not occurred yet. He speculated that this risk factor was the possibility of a devaluation of the Mexican peso. And sure enough, in August 1976 the peso was allowed to float against the dollar, and the peso promptly fell 46%.

1.2 Liquidity Risk—
The Peso Problem of Our Time

In this book, we argue that there was a peso problem during the period leading up to the global economic crisis of 2008-2009. And we also argue that it was an extremely pervasive peso problem, touching our entire society. It is present in every market (both financial and nonfinancial), it affects most financial institutions ranging from banks to hedge funds, it has always been there, and it will always continue to be there. This latent risk factor is *liquidity risk*.

Liquidity risk is a term widely used now in the popular press, but the truth is that few practitioners or academics seem to understand this risk well. Perhaps not surprisingly, because until just a few years ago, there was very little work being done to analyze this risk factor. The purpose of this book is not only to provide a detailed description of the concept of liquidity risk but also to lay out how this risk affects financial institutions and thereby gets transmitted into the global economic system. We do the latter by providing an analysis of the effects of three prominent liquidity risk events in the 20th century: 1) the Great Depression of the 1930s, 2) the collapse of the asset price bubble in Japan during the 1990s—often called the Lost Decade, and 3) the global economic crisis of 2008-2009, which, at the time of the writing of this book, many would argue is still continuing.

Before we get started, we provide a bit of additional motivation to study liquidity risk by presenting a couple of puzzles. These are some of the puzzles that initially prompted us to begin researching the concept of liquidity risk and its effects on financial institutions and the global economy.

1.3 WorldCom

WorldCom was one of the largest telecommunications companies in the world. Due to accounting fraud, in July 2002 the firm filed for bankruptcy. At the time it was the largest bankruptcy filing in the history of the United States.[2]

Figure 1.1 shows a time-series graph constructed using WorldCom's stock price movements over the two years prior to its bankruptcy. This graph depicts the assessment of WorldCom's probability of default[3]—or the risk that it would not pay its debt holders—by the equity markets over a period of time. The probability of default at any one point in time is calculated utilizing a widely used model known as the Merton model.[4] The only information being used in the calculations is data from the equity markets—no bond market information is used. Therefore, one can interpret Figure 1.1 as representing the equity market's probability of default assessment of WorldCom.

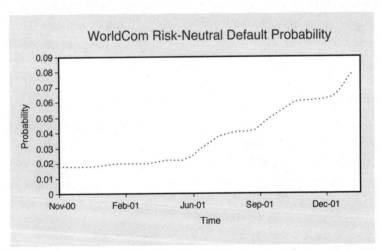

Figure 1.1   *Time series graph of WorldCom's default probability from the equity markets*

What we see from Figure 1.1 is that the equity markets start receiving information about trouble at WorldCom beginning in June 2001. From June 2001 to December 2001, the probability of default rises from approximately 2% to about 8%.

Figure 1.2 shows a time-series graph of credit spreads of a corporate bond that was issued by WorldCom in August 1998. A credit spread of a corporate bond is simply the bond's yield less the yield of a corresponding-maturity riskfree (Treasury) bond. Therefore, the credit spread is widely used by markets as an assessment of the likelihood of default of a corporate bond—the larger the credit spread, the higher the likelihood of default. Note that the credit spread of the WorldCom bond over the same time period as that in Figure 1.1 stays relatively flat at 1.8%. This indicates that the corporate bond market is assessing that WorldCom's probability of default has *not* changed.

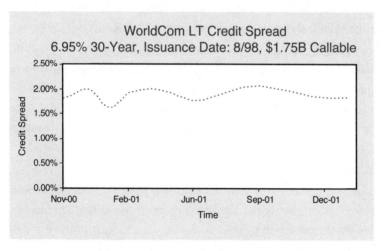

Figure 1.2 *Time series graph of WorldCom's credit spread*

This is a puzzle! How can the equity market and the corporate bond market be arriving at different assessments of WorldCom? The two markets should be getting identical information about

WorldCom. So, why does one market seemingly process this information differently and arrive at a different conclusion than the other market?

To answer this question, we have to understand what differences might exist between the equity market and bond market that might explain the divergent expectations. One major difference is the amount of liquidity and liquidity risk in the two markets. The U.S. corporate bond market is orders of magnitude less liquid than the U.S. equity market. As we will see, the difference in liquidity provides the key to explaining this puzzle.

1.4 Hedge Fund Returns

Hedge funds are an unregulated class of investment funds that became popular beginning in the late 1990s. At the end of 2010, the hedge fund industry managed more than $2 trillion.

Figure 1.3 contains a table of returns from the years 2000 thru 2008. The first column in this table denotes the year, and the next two columns compare the returns of a broad hedge fund index published by Credit Suisse/Tremont with the Standard & Poor's 500 stock index. For example, in 2003 the Tremont index produced a return of 15.46%, while the S&P 500 index produced a return of 28.69%.

Hedge funds charge relatively high fees compared to regulated funds, and one of the reasons they do so is their claim that the sophisticated hedging strategies they use produce returns that are insulated from stock market risk. Thus hedge funds produce positive returns whether the stock market is going up or down. Looking at Figure 1.3, we can verify this claim. During the years 2000-2002, the stock market declined a total of 38%.[5] During the same time period, the hedge fund index increased by 13%. So, it would appear that the hedge fund industry's fees were very much justified.

Year	HF Index	S&P 500
2000	4.84%	-9.10%
2001	4.41%	-11.89%
2002	3.05%	-22.10%
2003	15.46%	28.69%
2004	9.64%	10.88%
2005	7.60%	4.91%
2006	13.86%	15.79%
2007	12.58%	5.49%
2008	-19.07%	-38.49%

Figure 1.3   *Table of hedge fund returns and stock market returns*

In 2008, however, things change drastically. In this year, the stock market again dropped 38%, just like at the start of the decade. However, this time hedge funds produced a loss of 19% rather than the positive performance they produced earlier. This brings up an interesting question. What changed? Why did hedge funds produce a large negative performance in 2008 when the stock market dropped by the same amount?

The answer to this question lies in understanding the nature of the risk that hedge funds have on their balance sheets. As we show later in the book, hedge funds have considerable liquidity risk on their balance sheets, and this risk exposure is the key to explaining the performance difference of the hedge fund industry in 2008 versus the start of the decade.

1.5 The Structure of This Book

This book sets out to explain and discuss the questions and puzzles we just presented, using liquidity risk as a primary explanatory variable.

After this introductory chapter to liquidity, Chapter 2, "Liquidity Risk: Concepts," will define the key concepts surrounding the concept, such as liquidity cost, liquidity risk, and liquidity risk premium. We explore how financial institutions bear liquidity risk in their balance sheets. And we end the chapter with a discussion on how that affects financial institutions, especially banks, and the subsequent effects this has on the global economy.

In the three following chapters, we analyze three major historical liquidity shocks that occurred during the twentieth century. (There are many other examples during this time period, but we picked three of the most prominent ones.) We trace the shocks as they affect financial institutions and, subsequently, spread to the nonfinancial sector. In Chapter 3 we look at the United States Great Depression (1929-1933); in Chapter 4, we study Japan's Lost Decade of the 1990s; and in Chapter 5 we look at the United States Great Recession (2007-2009).

The book's final chapter, Chapter 6, explores the question of whether there are ways to lessen the effects of liqudity shocks, perhaps through public policy.

The book is written assuming that the reader has some familiarity with finance and economics. Concepts such as supply/demand equilibrium, bond yields, and option payoffs hopefully are not new.

Now, let's dive into the pool of liquidity risk.

Endnotes

1. Chairman's Letter, 2001 Berkshire Hathaway Annual Report, http://www. berkshirehathaway.com/2001ar/2001ar.pdf.

2. The record size of WorldCom's bankruptcy filing has been overtaken by the collapses of Lehman Brothers and Washington Mutual in 2008.

3. Technically, this is called the *risk-neutral probability of default*.

4. The Merton model says that a corporate bond is equivalent to a Treasury bond minus a put option on the assets of the firm, and that corporate equity is equivalent to a call option on the assets of the firm. For this calculation, we are using the latter approach. The implementation of this model is quite technical, and therefore, we do not delve into it in this book.

5. This calculation takes into account the compounding effect of the returns shown in Figure 1.3.

chapter 2

Liquidity Risk: Concepts

2.1 Introduction

Before we talk about financial institutions and the global economic system, we need to define the key concepts surrounding liquidity. In this chapter, we first define liquidity and the cost of liquidity, as well as introduce the concepts of liquidity risk and liquidity risk premium in the financial markets. We then explain how financial institutions ranging from banks and insurance companies to pension funds and hedge funds bear considerable liquidity risk in their balance sheets and why they choose to do so. Finally, we discuss the effects that bearing illiquidity risk has on financial institutions, especially banks, and the subsequent effects these have on the global economy.

2.2 What Is Liquidity?

The terms *liquidity* and *liquidity risk* have garnered a great deal of press recently as a result of the economic turmoil hitting the United States and Europe. These terms have a somewhat vague definition, however, and different people mean different things when using them. So before we explain what role liquidity, or more specifically the lack of liquidity, had on the economic crisis of 2008-2009, we should first explain what our definitions for liquidity, liquidity risk, and liquidity premium are.

While many people use the term *liquidity*, what they often mean is *illiquidity*. For example, when people say *liquidity risk*, they are referring to the risk of facing an illiquid market for a good or a financial security. Technically it would be more appropriate to refer to such risk as illiquidity risk because it is illiquidity that creates problems in the financial markets, not liquidity. However, it has become common among practitioners, in the popular press and even in academic circles, to simply use the terms liquidity risk and liquidity risk premium, so we will do so in this book as well. Keep in mind, however, that the risk being referred to is the likelihood of illiquidity.

Liquidity refers to how quickly and at what cost one can monetize an asset, whether that is a financial asset such as a stock or a real asset such as a commercial building. If one has an asset whose "true," or fundamental, value is $10, and one can instantly convert that asset into $10 of cash or cash equivalent, then we think of the market for that asset as perfectly liquid. Of course, such a perfectly liquid market is rarely observed in the world. Liquidity is also used to measure how quickly a buyer of an asset can convert cash into that tangible asset. So in a perfectly liquid market, someone who is looking to buy an asset whose fundamental value is $10 will be able to purchase that asset instantly for exactly $10 and receive it instantly.

There are two frictions that lead markets to be less than perfectly liquid, or *illiquid*. The first is an indirect cost. There is the possibility that it takes some amount of time before the conversion of the asset into $10 of cash takes place. For example, we may have to take the asset to a market, or if we are at the market, we may have to wait until someone comes along who wants the asset. This waiting time, sometimes referred to as a *waiting cost* or *search cost*, is one manifestation of illiquidity, and it makes a market less than perfectly liquid. The second friction is a direct cost. We may decide to pay someone a fee to get the asset sold immediately. Rather than paying the indirect cost of waiting until finding someone who will pay us the full $10 of cash, we may choose instead to cut our waiting time to zero and simply pay someone else, a "dealer," to do the waiting for us. We are essentially paying the dealer for *transaction immediacy*, or liquidity,[1] and therefore this cost is known as a *transaction cost* or *liquidity cost*.[2] For example, we may sell the asset to a dealer for $9.80 and let the dealer then worry about waiting to find someone who wants this asset. In this case, the dealer is providing us transaction immediacy in exchange for a fee of $0.20. While we have cut the waiting cost to zero, this is not a case of perfect liquidity because we have to pay a fee. While a dealer is a commonly used term for someone who provides such transaction immediacy (or liquidity) services in the financial markets, terms such as *principal, financial intermediary*, and *broker*[3] are also used. In the financial markets, financial institutions such as investment banks typically act as dealers for investors.

While in this book we stay focused on the financial markets, it is important to note that liquidity and the provision of liquidity in goods markets work in the same way as in financial markets. For example, when a customer goes to a store to buy toothpaste, the store is providing transaction immediacy to her in the toothpaste market, that is, it is allowing her immediate access to purchasing toothpaste rather than having to wait and find a toothpaste seller, or manufacturer, herself. Similarly, the store is providing liquidity to the toothpaste manufacturer as well. By purchasing the toothpaste from the manufacturer and carrying it on its own shelves (and balance sheet), the store is sparing the manufacturer from having to go out and find customers for the toothpaste that it owns. So for both the customer and the toothpaste manufacturer, the store is providing transaction immediacy: It allows both the customer and the manufacturer to immediately have a transaction (buying in the customer's case, and selling in the case of the manufacturer). Note, however, that the transaction immediacy is not occurring at the same time for both the customer and the manufacturer. Therefore, the store must carry the toothpaste on its own balance sheet between the time that it purchases the toothpaste from the manufacturer and the time that the customer purchases the toothpaste from the store. Thus, just like a financial dealer the store is using its balance sheet to bridge the time between the manufacturer and the customer. It is this bridging function that creates transaction immediacy, or liquidity, for both the customer and the manufacturer, and we can say therefore that the store is providing liquidity services in toothpaste.

An important characteristic about trading illiquid assets is that there is a tradeoff between waiting cost and liquidity cost. If an investor is willing to do some searching (and therefore waiting) before buying or selling an asset, the investor can lower the amount of liquidity cost he pays. If an investor is willing to wait as long as it takes to find a counterparty himself, then he will pay zero transaction cost, but he will pay a full waiting cost (though the waiting cost is uncertain). At the other limit, if an investor is not willing to wait at all, that is, if he wants an immediate transaction, he will pay zero waiting cost but a full transaction cost. For example, suppose a homeowner wants to sell a home. If she wants to sell a home immediately (within three days, for example), then she would have to discount the home considerably to get this transaction done—low waiting cost, but high liquidity cost. However, if the homeowner is willing to wait up to a year, then she does not need to discount the home very much, if at all, to sell the home within that time period—low liquidity cost, but high waiting cost.

Another characteristic to note about illiquid assets is the way in which a dealer collects his fee for providing transaction immediacy services (or liquidity services) to customers. In the example of the store selling toothpaste, it buys the toothpaste from the manufacturer at slightly below the fundamental value of the toothpaste. Say the store buys it at $3 per tube, and we assume a fundamental value of $3.25 per tube. The store then sells to the customer at slightly above the fundamental value of the toothpaste, say $3.50 per tube (see Figure 2.1). In this way a fee for providing transaction immediacy to both the manufacturer and customer is built into the transaction price that each sees. This is why this fee is often referred to as a transaction cost. The financial markets work the same way. Instead of toothpaste, the asset might be a stock. Then, the $3 price would be referred to as a *bid* price, and the $3.50 price would be referred to as an *ask* price. The difference between these two prices, $0.50, is commonly called a *bid-ask spread*, and this is the security dealer's fee for providing transaction immediacy. It is for this reason that the terms *transaction cost* and *bid-ask spread* are used interchangeably.

Figure 2.1   *Illustration of dealing function and fees*

2.3 Model of Liquidity Costs

The immediate question at this stage normally is what is an appropriate or fair transaction cost, or liquidity cost. Do we have a model for determining a fair liquidity cost for an asset? The answer is that many such models exist. Every dealer has its own model of some sort (and some of these models are more qualitative than quantitative) for determining a liquidity cost for an asset in a specific market.

For the purposes of this book, we discuss one model of liquidity costs: the CJS model.[4] This is not the first model of liquidity costs ever derived, nor will it be the last. We present it because it is highly representative of the types of quantitative models that have been created and used by dealers to calculate liquidity costs. The CJS model itself is fairly technical as its foundations lie in option pricing theory. We do not delve into the technical details of the CJS model but instead we focus on the features of this model that are found in virtually all liquidity cost models.

Figure 2.2 presents a graph of some output from the CJS model. This graph is called the quantity structure of bid and ask prices for a security. The horizontal axis of the graph shows the amount of a security to be traded (bought or sold), in this case how many shares of a stock that are to be traded. The vertical axis of the graph displays the price at which a dealer would do the buy or sell transaction. Essentially this graph displays the buy and sell price at a point in time that a dealer would quote to an investor for any given amount of a security that the investor wished to trade. The buy price, or bid price, is given by the lower curve in the graph, and the sell price, or ask price, is given by the upper curve. For example, the quantity structure of prices in this figure indicates that at the current moment this dealer would be willing to buy 1,000 shares of the stock from an investor at $19.80 per share, or he would be willing to sell 1,000 shares of the stock to any investor at $20.20 per share. The $0.40 difference between these two prices is the bid-ask spread for transacting 1,000 shares. Moving to the right on the horizontal axis, we find that the same dealer currently would be willing to buy 3,500 shares of this stock from any investor for $19.60 per share or sell 3,500 shares to any investor for $20.40 per share.

In Figure 2.2 the price of $20 per share is the fundamental value of this security, but notice that this price would never lead to a trade; it is not a transactable price for any buyer or seller. An investor always buys from a dealer at above the fundamental value of a security and sells to a dealer at below fundamental value of a security. This buy-sell price gap is the bid-ask spread—it is basically the liquidity cost of this security. As noted earlier, this cost represents the compensation the dealer wants for providing transaction immediacy to an investor, that is, it is the fee paid to the dealer to do the waiting for a buy or sell counterparty rather than an investor having to do the waiting himself.

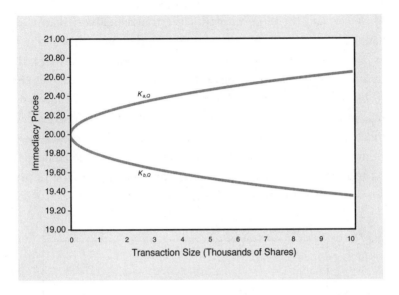

Figure 2.2 *Quantity structure of bid and ask prices*

Figure 2.2 teaches us a number of things about the general properties of liquidity costs. The first thing it shows us is that as we try to transact a larger and larger quantity of securities, the liquidity cost increases. The reason for this is that the dealer who is acting as the counterparty will need to wait longer if it has more of the security it has to buy or sell. For example, if we sell the dealer a lot of shares, it will take longer for the dealer to find counterparties to offload these shares. During this time, the shares are sitting on the dealer's balance sheet, which uses up the dealer's capital and is risky.[5] The longer the dealer has to hold on to these shares, the more it needs to charge in bid-ask spread to make up for these *inventory costs*. This is a common characteristic of dealers in both financial and goods markets.

A natural extension of this characteristic is that the more buyers and sellers arriving in the market to transact, that is, the more order flow there is in a security, the shorter the expected waiting time for the dealer, and therefore the lower the transaction cost that it will charge. In Figure 2.3, for example, we take the same stock and market parameters that were used in Figure 2.2 and simply increase the buy and sell order flow that the dealer is experiencing. As one can see, the bid-ask spread decreases at all transaction sizes. The increased buy and sell demand means there is less waiting time for the dealer to offload a position in his inventory. Less waiting time means lower inventory costs to the dealer, and it therefore requires less compensation to cover these costs. The lower required compensation in turn allows it to charge a lower bid-ask spread.

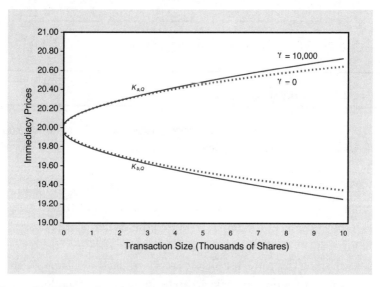

Figure 2.3 *Effect of an order flow increase on quantity structure of bid/ask prices*

Another important property of bid-ask spreads is that they can become asymmetric, as seen in Figure 2.4. This asymmetry results if the dealer experiences more of one type of order flow—for example, more sell order flow than buy order flow. In this case, which is precisely the one depicted in Figure 2.4, the dealer's inventory is increasing because there are more sellers than buyers of the security. The dealer is buying more from the sellers than it is selling to the buyers. In response to this order imbalance, the dealer starts to buy at lower prices from sellers to dissuade some sellers and thereby slow down, and hopefully reverse, the inventory accumulation it has experienced. The dealer also sells to buyers at lower prices to encourage more buyers, which again should help slow down or reverse the inventory accumulation. This results in asymmetric bid and ask prices around the fundamental value of the security. It also results in a higher overall bid-ask spread, which is the extra compensation to the dealer for the increased inventory it is being forced to carry.

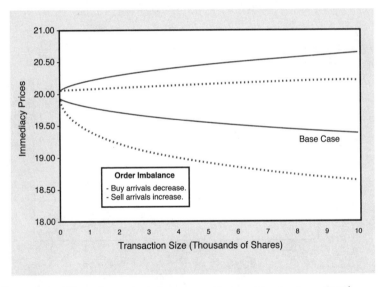

Figure 2.4 *Effect of an order imbalance on the quantity structure of bid/ask prices*

The key determinant of the bid-ask spread that a dealer charges is the amount of risk that he takes in holding a security as inventory. A long waiting time before a security is taken out of his inventory means greater risk for the dealer. Another important determinant of risk is the volatility of a security's price.[6] If the price of a security is highly volatile, then for any given inventory holding period, there is a greater chance that the dealer could lose a large amount of money. This higher risk means that the dealer has to hold more capital against the inventory, which means higher capital costs.[7] The dealer then has to recover these higher capital costs through a higher bid-ask spread. Figure 2.5 illustrates this case. In this figure, we begin with the output from Figure 2.2 and keep all parameters except for an increase in the stock volatility, from 25% per annum to 37.5%. This increased volatility results in a higher bid-ask spread at all transaction sizes as the dealer attempts to cover the increased capital costs arising from the increase in his inventory volatility.

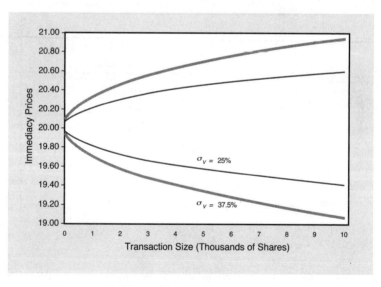

Figure 2.5 *Effect of a volatility shock on the quantity structure of bid/ask prices*

One may ask what is the role of new information in the determination of the quantity structure of prices. For example, if IBM reports unexpected good news, which causes the market to revise upward the future cashflows of the firm, how would this impact the quantity structure of prices? The answer is that information such as this does not affect the quantity structure of prices for a security—it affects the level of the fundamental value of the security.[8] The bid and ask curves for a security are only affected by the order flow rate and any imbalance in this order flow rate, as well as the volatility of fundamental value of the security.

2.4 Liquidity Risk and Liquidity Shocks

In Figure 2.6 we put the preceding characteristics together to illustrate one of the most important concepts in this book. Figure 2.6 illustrates a *liquidity shock* or *liquidity crisis* occurring in the market for a security. In such an event we have two important things occurring at the same time. First, order flow becomes highly asymmetric with the dealer facing significantly more sellers than buyers. The dashed line shows the effect of this order imbalance on the quantity structure of bid and ask prices. Bid prices and ask prices decrease, creating asymmetric curves around the fundamental value of the security. Second, the security's price volatility increases substantially. The increase in volatility greatly amplifies the effect of the order imbalance resulting in a hugely asymmetric quantity structure of bid and ask prices around the fundamental value of the security. The second solid line shows the result of the amplification effect of increased volatility. In this example, for transaction sizes of 10,000 shares a seller is only able to sell at prices that are 10% lower than the fundamental value of the security—that is an enormous decrease in the price of the security to the seller. What is happening is that the volatility increase greatly amplifies the increased inventory costs the dealer faces due to the order imbalance. The dealer as a result has to take drastic action to cover his inventory costs and does so by radically dropping the price at which he is willing to buy from sellers. In real world financial markets this huge increase in liquidity cost would in turn cause buy and sell volume to decrease substantially. With sellers still outnumbering buyers (due to the initial order imbalance that started the liquidity shock), we would witness more transactions occurring on the lower curve in Figure 2.6, the bid curve. While the fundamental price of the security has not changed, the prices we see coming out of the market are only those from actual transactions. With more transactions occurring on the lower curve in Figure 2.6, it would appear to everyone that the price that the security is trading at has dropped significantly. Thus, a liquidity shock is a dramatic increase in the price volatility of a security and a dramatic decrease in trading volume with more sellers than buyers for the security, and it leads to a dramatic decrease in the price of the security.

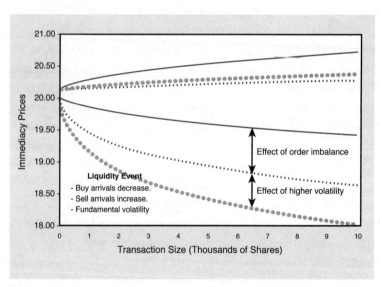

Figure 2.6   *Order imbalance + Volatility Increase = Liquidity Shock*

An example of a liquidity shock occurred in late August 2006 in the natural gas futures market. During the last week of August, the September futures contract for natural gas (a contract that called for delivery of 10,000 million BTU, British Thermal Units, of natural gas at the start of September) experienced a substantial liquidity shock. During this week, the futures price associated with that contract fell from $8 per million BTU to slightly less than $6.50. This represented a drop of nearly 20% in one week. At the same time, implied volatility on gas options (an indicator of price volatility in this market) went from approximately 25% to more than 90%. This also corresponded to a complete drying up of liquidity in this contract as one hedge fund, which was trying to sell this contract, found itself accounting for more than half of the trading volume at the New York Mercantile Exchange (NYMEX) and the Intercontinental Exchange (ICE). The name of this fund was Amaranth. Due to the substantial liquidity-related losses it incurred in trading this contract and a few others, the fund lost $6.5 billion (out of the approximately $10 billion in assets it managed just prior to this week) during this week and the first two weeks of September. The cause of the liquidity shock in this case was the sudden selling of the September contract that Amaranth had to do. However, Amaranth owned so many of the total open positions (approximately 60%) in this futures contract on the NYMEX and ICE that its selling completely overwhelmed the trading volume in this contract, causing the bid curve for this contract to decline substantially.

Liquidity shocks occur regularly for individual securities in the market. They are mostly minor shocks but occasionally major ones like the previous example. However, sometimes liquidity shocks occur on a marketwide basis, and this is what we refer to as a systematic liquidity shock.[9] The main characteristics of a marketwide liquidity shock are the same as those of a liquidity shock to an individual security. The market experiences substantial asymmetry in order flow with sellers far outnumbering the buyers, which results in substantially lower bid curves for all securities. Because there is far more selling than buying, most transactions that occur, and therefore are reported, are sell transactions, which leads to significant reported price declines of all securities in the market. There is also substantially higher price volatility in the market, due mostly to the bid and ask curves being much wider.[10] As we show later, the financial crisis during the Fall of 2008 was a marketwide liquidity shock that affected multiple markets including equities and most fixed income markets throughout the world. Even some of the most liquid markets in the world such as the Over-the-Counter (OTC) market for interest rate swaps saw severe declines in bid curves and trading volume.

One of the most important risks that an investor takes when buying any security or asset is the risk of a liquidity shock. More broadly, when buying any security or asset, an investor bears liquidity risk—the risk of movements of the bid and ask curves of a security. A liquidity shock is simply the special case of an extreme movement in the bid and ask curves, particularly the bid curve.

In general, when an investor buys any risky asset, he is taking two types of risk. The first type of risk is known as market risk. This risk really deals with the risk of movements in the fundamental value of an asset. Examples of market risk include news about a firm's operating margins, news about GDP growth, news about Federal Reserve interest rate policy, and so on. All of these would cause the market to revise their fundamental valuation of an asset[11] independent of how an asset is traded or its transaction cost. In return for bearing market risk, an investor is compensated by earning a market risk premium. This premium is in the form of extra expected return above the riskfree rate. The market risk premium for holding U.S. equities, for example, is widely believed to be approximately 5% per annum. This means that an investor would earn on average about 5% plus the current long-run Treasury bond yield per year by holding a diversified basket of U.S. equities such as the S&P 500 for a long period of time. Of course, some securities are more sensitive to market risk than others; that is, some securities move more than others when a piece of news comes out. It is common practice in finance to use a sensitivity measure called "market beta" to measure the sensitivity of a particular security to some market news. A market beta of 1 is considered to be average market risk, while higher market betas reflect higher market risk and lower betas reflect lower market risk. For example, utility stocks have low beta because regardless of what happens in the world or the economy, people will still use water, electricity, gas, and so on. Therefore utility stocks move very little to market news. Luxury retailers on the other hand have very high beta because spending on luxury goods comes out of people's discretionary spending, which is highly sensitive to economic conditions.

The second type of risk an investor faces is movements in the bid and ask curves for an asset. A liquidity shock is an example of this risk. Essentially liquidity risk is the risk that an investor needs to buy or sell an asset at a particular point in time but that the bid and/or ask curves at that point in time just happen to be unfavorable, resulting in a large transaction cost to him. Every asset in the world, from a financial security to a piece of commercial property to a barrel of oil, has this risk built in. Therefore, as with market risk, an investor must be compensated for bearing this risk. We call this compensation a *liquidity risk premium.*

2.5 Liquidity Risk Premium

A natural question then is how much is this liquidity risk premium. We'll start, though, with how we determine the market risk premium. We usually do this by measuring the performance of a market, for example the equity market, over a long period of time and then subtract out the yield of a long-maturity Treasury bond. The S&P 500 index, for example, has returned about 9% per year over the last hundred years. The current 30-year Treasury bond yield is about 4%. This leads to a market risk premium of 9%-4% = 5% per annum.[12] This is the market risk premium for taking an amount of market risk equal to a market beta of 1. If a U.S. equity investor holds a portfolio with a market risk equal to a market beta of 2, he would expect to earn a market premium of 10% on that portfolio. Holding a portfolio with a market beta of 0.5 would lead to an expected market premium of 2.5% on that portfolio.

Now, to determine the liquidity risk premium, we would like to follow a similar procedure. However, this is not as easy because we cannot directly buy a basket of liquidity from the markets and then measure its long-term performance as we just did with equities. We need to use a bit of financial engineering to construct this basket of liquidity.

Figure 2.7 shows the balance sheet for a fund (we will call it the Liquidity Premium Fund) that we will construct to isolate and hold liquidity risk. If we construct it well, we should be able to simply measure the long-run performance of this fund to determine the liquidity risk premium. We construct this fund using U.S. corporate bonds. The reason we use corporate bonds is simply that we need to find a market where liquidity risk is substantial. The most well-known markets, the U.S. equity market and the U.S. Treasury market, are both very liquid markets in comparison to most other markets around the world. By contrast, the U.S. corporate bond market is a relatively illiquid market—the median U.S. corporate bond issue trades only once per year as compared to the median U.S. equity, which trades about once every few seconds. What we will do in constructing this fund is to go long and short corporate bonds in such a way as to keep liquidity risk and hedge out all other risks. That way, we isolate liquidity risk.

In the balance sheet in Figure 2.7, we start by putting $100 into the fund—this is denoted on the balance sheet by "Equity Capital." We then buy $100 worth of 1,000 different corporate bonds that are relatively illiquid and therefore have a high degree of liquidity risk.

This is denoted by "Long Bonds." We also short sell $100 worth of 1,000 different corporate bonds that are relatively liquid in comparison to the bonds that we just bought on the asset side of the fund; so, these bonds have relatively low liquidity risk. This is denoted by "Short Bonds." We measure liquid and illiquid here by trading volume. It follows that each of the bonds on the asset side of the balance sheet has higher trading volume than each of the bonds on the liability side of the balance sheet. We receive $100 of cash from short selling $100 worth of bonds. This cash is simply invested in short-term Treasury bills but is denoted as "Cash" on the balance sheet.

"Liquidity Premium" Fund

$100 Cash	$100 Short Bonds
$100 Long Bonds	$100 Equity Capital

Figure 2.7 *Balance sheet for a fund constructed to earn a liquidity premium*

The long bond positions and the short bond positions are also chosen in a special way beyond just having low liquidity and high liquidity, respectively. Corporate bonds have other risk factors beyond just liquidity risk. They have default risk and interest rate risk. If the probability of default of the issuing company increases, the bond price will decrease. Similarly, if interest rates in the U.S. economy increase, then bond prices will decrease. Because we want to only have liquidity risk in this fund and no other risk exposures, we have to hedge out the default and interest rate risk of the long and short bonds. We do this by choosing the long and short bond positions such that the default risk and interest rate risk of the two offset each other. To do this we choose the long and short positions to be of the same credit quality, that is, the same default risk.[13] Because the left-hand side

(LHS) of the balance sheet is long this default risk and the right-hand side (RHS) is short this same amount of default risk, the default risks cancel each other out. Thus, the balance sheet as it is constructed now has no default risk in it. Similarly, we go long and short bonds that have the same duration, that is, the same interest rate risk.[14] Once again, because the LHS is long this interest rate risk and the RHS is short this interest rate risk, the interest rate risks cancel each other out. Thus by having the same amount of default risk and interest rate risk on both the asset and liability side of the balance sheet, these two risks cancel out and the fund is no longer exposed to these risk factors.[15]

Because LHS of the balance sheet has illiquid bonds and the right-hand side (RHS) of the balance sheet has liquid bonds, liquidity risk is not cancelled out.[16] As a result, liquidity risk is the only remaining risk factor in the fund, and the equity of the fund is exposed to this risk factor. Just as with market risk, the performance of the equity of this fund over a long period of time reflects the compensation for taking liquidity risk, that is, the fund's long-run performance is the liquidity risk premium.

Figure 2.8 contains the performance of the equity of this fund— the return for holding liquidity risk in a portfolio. The value of the equity starts out at $100 and changes as liquidity conditions in the bond market change. The first thing to note is that the average performance of this liquidity risk fund, or factor, is about 7.8% per annum. Because the fund's long-run performance is precisely the liquidity risk premium, we can conclude that the liquidity risk premium is about 7.8% per annum. This is greater than the market risk premium that we estimated earlier of 5%. Just as we do with the market risk premium, we set this amount of liquidity premium as a benchmark and denote this as the amount of liquidity premium earned for taking an amount of liquidity risk that is equal to a liquidity beta of 1. A liquidity beta of 2 would earn 15.6%, and so on. The liquidity beta of equity markets in the United States is about 0.1, a fairly low value indicating that the equity markets have little liquidity risk. This value would indicate that out of the total premium an investor earns for holding equities, about 0.1 x 7.8% = 0.8% is actually compensation for taking liquidity risk.

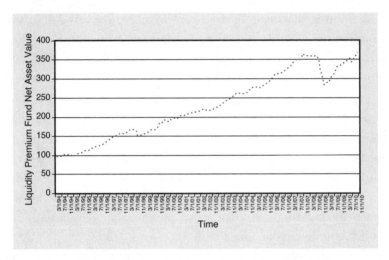

Figure 2.8   *Net asset value of a fund invested only in liquidity risk*

Another interesting thing to note is the major decrease in the liquidity fund during the 2008-2009 economic recession. For such a decrease to occur, the value of the LHS of the balance sheet has to drop more than the RHS drops, that is, the value of illiquid assets has to drop more than the value that liquid assets drop. As shown in Figure 2.9, this is precisely what happens when there is a liquidity shock. Therefore, this sharp decrease in the liquidity fund tells us that there was a major liquidity shock during this recession (in fact, we will argue later that the liquidity shock was the main cause of this recession and subsequent stagnation). Compare the performance of the liquidity fund during this period to the performance of the fund during the 2001-2002 recession. During the 2001-2002 recession the liquidity fund increased in value rather than decreasing. This indicates that the 2001-2002 recession, like most past recessions, was very different from the 2008-2009 recession: The 2001-2002 recession was not the result of a liquidity shock nor were there any liquidity shocks around or during this time period. In fact, to find the last major liquidity shock in the financial markets, one has to go back to Fall 1998—during the Long Term Capital Management crisis—but this shock did not lead to a recession. The last major liquidity shock that led to a recession in the United States was during the later 1980s and early 1990s—the Savings & Loan crisis.

We are now in a position to take a short diversion and solve one of the puzzles posed in Chapter 1, "Motivation for Understanding Liquidity Risk." This is the WorldCom puzzle as to why the corporate bond market and the equity market seemingly had opposite views of WorldCom's prospects. Why did the equity market predict an increase in the probability of default for WorldCom while the bond market seemingly indicated no change in the probability of default for WorldCom (by letting the credit spread of WorldCom bonds to remain unchanged, as shown in Figure 2.10)? To answer this, one has to remember that liquidity risk is an important part of the total risk of any corporate bond (whereas it is only a small part of the risk of an equity security). Therefore the aggregate credit spread of any corporate bond represents compensation for both default risk as well as liquidity risk. We can use the liquidity factor from Figure 2.8 to help separate out the part of WorldCom's corporate bond yield due to liquidity risk from the part that is due to default risk.[17] Figure 2.11 contains a time-series graph of both the default spread and the liquidity spread. What we see from this graph is that, in fact, the default spread did increase. This increase in the default spread, however, did not show up in the aggregate credit spread for WorldCom because it was offset by a decrease in the liquidity spread (the aggregate credit spread is the sum of the default spread and the liquidity spread). In early July 2001, WorldCom conducted the largest corporate bond issuance in the history of the U.S. financial markets. This issuance made all WorldCom corporate bonds substantially more liquid. The increased liquidity resulted in liquidity spreads dropping for WorldCom, as we see in Figure 2.11, which offset the increased default spread. Therefore, the equity and bond market were not out of sync with each other—they both predicted increased default risk for WorldCom.

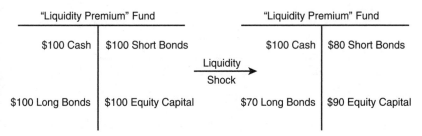

Figure 2.9   *Result of a liquidity shock on the Liquidity Premium Fund*

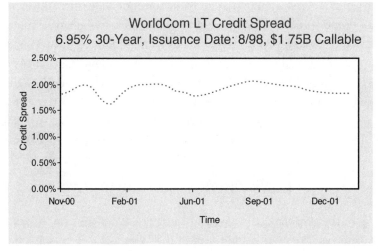

Figure 2.10   *Time series graph of the credit spread for a WorldCom bond issue*

31

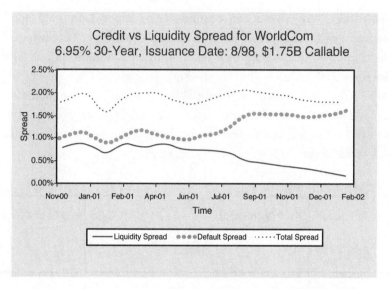

Figure 2.11 *Time series of default spread versus liquidity spread for WorldCom bond*

What this puzzle teaches us is to never use the aggregate credit spread of a corporate bond as an indicator of default risk. The aggregate credit spread is composed of both a default spread and liquidity spread, and the liquidity spread needs to be separated out to isolate the default spread in order to form conclusions about the chances of default of a bond issuer. In fact, several academic papers indicate that on average nearly half the aggregate credit spread for corporate bonds is really due to the liquidity spread, but there is substantial variation of this proportion across the cross-section of U.S. corporate bonds.

2.6 Why Bear Liquidity Risk?

One of the obvious questions at this point is of course why would an investor want to bear liquidity risk if the expected return is not substantially higher than that of bearing market risk. To answer this question, it is important to keep in mind what each of these two risks represents. Market risk represents uncertainty in the movements of the fundamental value of a security. Liquidity risk represents uncertainty in the movements of the bid and ask curves in the quantity structure of prices of the security. Market risk is a risk that is not easy to avoid—anytime one buys any asset, there is a chance that new information relevant to the pricing of the asset appears and changes the fundamental value of the asset.[18] Liquidity risk is only a risk if one is going to transact in a security because only then are the bid or ask curves for the security relevant—at all other times, only the fundamental value of the security (and, therefore, market risk) is relevant.

If an investor has a long investment horizon for an asset and therefore does not plan on selling the asset for a long time, liquidity risk is irrelevant to him. If an investor will not be selling an asset for several years, for example, the risk of the movement of bid and ask curves for that asset in the intervening years does not matter. However, suppose the markets are pricing the asset so that it pays a liquidity premium. Suppose that the asset has a liquidity beta of 0.5, so that the investor is earning an extra $0.5 \times 7.8\% = 3.9\%$ in addition to the market risk premium. Then this liquidity risk premium is earned without taking much real liquidity risk because of the investor's plans not to sell the asset for a long time. Thus, the investor's long investment horizon makes the liquidity premium that the markets are paying to anyone willing to bear the liquidity risk in the asset into "free money," or an arbitrage, for the investor.[19] When investors invest into such asset classes as private equity, venture capital, real estate, infrastructure, and hedge funds, they are taking substantial liquidity risk because it is difficult to sell the holdings of these funds quickly, that is, the bid curve is steep to begin with and will drop substantially for most assets being held in these types of funds if the investment manager tries to sell them quickly. This also indicates that the liquidity beta of these funds is very high—in fact they are greater than 1. That is why these funds have the potential to generate much higher returns than typical mutual funds—the liquidity risk premium easily adds 10% or more to the inherent market risk premium earned by these funds.[20] These asset classes have a special name due to the illiquidity of their components; they are called *alternative investments*.

Alternative investments have the potential to generate high returns due to the substantial liquidity risk premia embedded in the assets. However, an investor must have a long investment horizon to ensure that the returns from these investments have a high "Sharpe ratio," that is, generate a high return per unit of total risk (market plus liquidity risk) taken. If the investor is forced to liquidate these assets prematurely, it can be extremely costly.

2.7 Liquidity-Driven Investing (LqDI)

There is an investment approach used by many institutional investors that have liability streams to capitalize on liquidity risk premiums in financial markets. No widely used name exists for the paradigm, so we will call it simply *liquidity-driven investing*, or LqDI.[21] As shown later, this investment approach creates an important risk exposure on the balance sheets of most financial institutions.

We use a pension fund as an example to demonstrate the principle of LqDI. A pension fund is a financial institution that exists to pay retirees a fixed income stream during their retired lives. Therefore, a pension fund has a stream of liabilities, or obligations, that it faces: the current and future payments that it is required to make to retirees. It also has assets to meet this stream: the accumulated pension contributions made by the employer (and that have not been paid out yet to retirees). These pension assets need to be invested in such a way that the pension fund can meet all of its current and future obligations. Additionally, the pension sponsor, the employer or union, usually wants the returns to be high to reduce the future required pension contributions. However, it also wants the risk to be low so that there is no risk of a shortfall in the pension fund, which would force the sponsor to make extra contributions into the pension fund.

With the LqDI approach, the pension assets needed to make payments to retirees over the short term, for example the next ten years, are not invested into risky securities. No matter what happens in the financial markets or the global economy, these payments must be made. The pension fund cannot legally or ethically tell a retiree that the annual pension payment that was promised to her cannot be made during the current year because financial markets performed poorly. So, the pension assets needed for meeting these short-term pension liabilities are invested in safe assets: government bonds or equivalent fixed income instruments that are duration-matched to the short-term liabilities.

Once the near-term liability stream is taken care of—that is, matched—the pension fund needs to decide how to invest the remaining pension assets. With these assets, the fund can take investment risk to earn a potentially higher return and possibly reduce the future pension contributions of the plan sponsor. This investment risk comes in the form of market risk. However, the fund also has a competitive advantage it can utilize. With near-term liabilities matched, all remaining pension assets can be invested with a long investment horizon in mind. From our earlier discussion, this means the pension can take liquidity risk without it really being too much of a risk. Therefore, the pension fund invests to obtain both market and liquidity risk with its remaining pension assets. As much as possible it tries to invest in alternative investments because these asset classes provide substantial liquidity risk in addition to market risk.

However, the pension fund cannot invest entirely in alternative investments with its remaining assets. This is because there is a chance that a sudden, unanticipated need for cash arises. This could occur because of mistakes the pension fund made in calculating its lia-bility stream, imperfect duration matching of the short-term liabili-ties, or unexpected legal, regulatory, or administrative costs. For these reasons, some of the investments into risky assets are allocated to asset classes that provide only market risk and no liquidity risk. Thus, if an unexpected shortfall occurs for any reason in meeting the short-term liability stream, these assets can be sold quickly to raise cash. Financial instruments that trade in liquid public markets are ideal. Examples include large capitalization stocks in both the United States and other well-developed countries, sovereign bonds of well-devel-oped countries, and commodities.

Figure 2.12 shows a result of the LqDI process on a pension fund balance sheet. A pension fund following an LqDI strategy first uses the pension assets to match its short-term liability stream with high-quality fixed income instruments—we denote these as Tier 1 assets. It then creates a small safety buffer for these short-term liability streams by investing a small amount of the remaining pension assets into investments with market risk but no liquidity risk—Tier 2 assets. Then all remaining assets are invested into alternative investments to earn both a market risk premium and liquidity risk premium—Tier 3 assets.

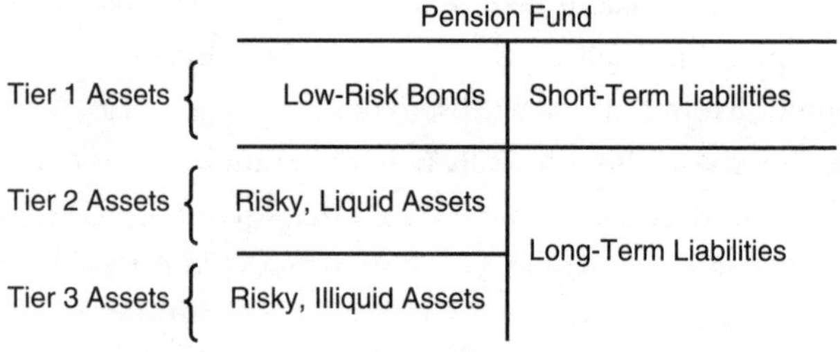

	Pension Fund	
Tier 1 Assets {	Low-Risk Bonds	Short-Term Liabilities
Tier 2 Assets {	Risky, Liquid Assets	Long-Term Liabilities
Tier 3 Assets {	Risky, Illiquid Assets	

Figure 2.12   *Result of LqDI process for a pension fund balance sheet*

Many other financial institutions beyond pension funds utilize this LqDI approach. This approach is widely used by endowments.

The liability stream for a university endowment is the annual contributions it is expected to make to a university's operating budget. However, because most universities' operating budgets grow predictably, these expected annual contributions are similar to the payments that a pension fund is required to make to its retirees—they can be calculated fairly precisely far out into the future. In such a situation, the LqDI approach described previously for the example pension fund is ideal for an endowment as well, and most endowment funds use this approach.

The LqDI approach is also widely followed by foundations. In the case of foundations, the liability stream is the charitable giving that the foundation does. While a bit less predictable than an endowment fund's contribution to a university operating budget, this can nevertheless be calculated fairly precisely for a good ways into the future. Therefore, the LqDI approach works well and is commonly utilized by foundations.

The LqDI approach is also utilized by insurance companies. The liability of an insurance company is a claim made by a policyholder, such as someone who holds a life insurance policy. Because it is uncertain when a policyholder will make a claim—for example, it is difficult to know when a policyholder who has life insurance will die—the liability associated with an individual *is not* predictable. This would appear to make LqDI infeasible for insurance companies. However, if an insurance company writes insurance policies to many individuals of varying types (age, sex, marital status, ethnicity, and so on), the collective payments that need to be made every year to this pool of people *is* highly predictable. So even though it is difficult to predict the chances of any individual policyholder filing a claim, it is easy to predict how many policyholders within a pool of people will file a claim during a given period of time—doing this is one of the main jobs of actuaries within an insurance company. This means that if an insurance company writes policies to a diverse enough pool of people, the liability stream of the insurance company becomes predictable. This is precisely the strategy that all insurance companies follow in most of their product lines. As a result, the LqDI approach becomes applicable and is widely practiced by the insurance industry.

However, note that the insurance company runs a risk that the liability stream does not follow the pattern predicted by the actuarial tables. Specifically, it runs the risk that it faces a lump-sum set of claims, that is, that a large number of claims are made at the same time. In such a scenario, the insurance company would have to start selling its liquid securities: its Tier 2 assets. If the claims it faces are even greater than the Tier 2 assets, it would then be forced to start selling highly illiquid Tier 3 assets, thereby incurring large liquidity-related losses—essentially, the insurance company has now become a distressed seller. The firm may use up all of its equity capital as it incurs these losses and be forced out of business. The only way to protect against this scenario is to make sure there are no lump-sum claims, and the best (though not perfect) way to ensure this is to write insurance policies to a hugely diverse pool of customers.[22]

The insured losses from Hurricane Katrina, which made landfall in southeast Louisiana in late August 2005, provide a good example of lump-sum claims. This event resulted in the largest ever set of insured losses for the insurance industry (approximately $41 billion). If an insurance company had written too many property insurance policies in southeast Louisiana, its capital would have easily been wiped out due to the fact that loss claims would have all come in at the same time. However, no insurer was bankrupted by the claims from this event. Every insurer realizes that natural disaster events will result in lump-sum claims. So insurers make sure that the property insurance they write to any one region is a small percentage of their total insurance portfolio. In addition, many insurance companies choose to "reinsure" the policies they have written. In other words, many insurance companies sell off part of the policies they have written in a region to other insurance companies or institutional investors.[23] Reinsurance is the main reason why no insurers went out of business due to claims from Hurricane Katrina. Reinsurance has become a major segment of the insurance industry, and it is one of the major tools that allow insurance companies to keep their insurance portfolios well-diversified.

Another example of lump-sum claims is the losses that the U.S. insurer American International Group (AIG) took when the market for collateralized debt obligations (CDOs) declined in value in 2008. Essentially, AIG had written insurance to investors in these CDOs.[24] AIG was assuming that all the various CDOs it had written insurance on would never decline in value all at the same time, which would have resulted in lump-sum claims. They felt certain that they had a well-diversified insurance portfolio. By mid-2008, it had written more than $500 billion in this form of insurance. Unfortunately for AIG, by Fall 2008 the entire CDO market had declined considerably in value, which made it likely that AIG would be facing a large set of claims all at the same time. As a result, many investors that had purchased insurance from AIG required AIG to put up additional collateral on the insurance policies (to ensure that AIG would make good on the claims if they were filed). Due to the size of AIG's CDO insurance portfolio, and the likelihood of lump-sum claims, AIG's credit ratings were lowered by the major credit rating agencies. This made it impossible for AIG to issue debt and raise funds to post as collateral. As a result, AIG had to be bailed out by the Federal Reserve, one of the largest bailouts of a private firm in the history of the United States.

Commercial banks also use the LqDI approach. Like insurance companies, the liability stream of a commercial bank does not seem predictable. The liabilities of a commercial bank are primarily deposits. Once a customer puts money into the bank, part or all of that deposit can be withdrawn at any time, and the bank must make the funds immediately available upon a withdrawal request. This deposit is therefore a liability, and a single customer's withdrawal pattern is difficult to predict. However, as with insurance the withdrawal pattern is much easier to predict for a large pool of depositors than for a single individual. Therefore, banks focus on getting deposits from a large and diversified pool of customers. Once it has this large pool, the liability stream for the bank becomes much more predictable, and once again the bank can use an LqDI approach. Due to bank regulations,[25] banks cannot easily invest into alternative investments. Instead, banks invest their Tier 3 assets into other types of illiquid instruments such as commercial loans and real estate loans; that is, they lend money.

Commercial banks also borrow, or issue debt, in addition to taking in deposits. This is another important source of financing, and the funds from these debt proceeds are also used for investments, just like the funds from deposits. The liability structure of the debt, however, is much simpler than that of deposits because the maturity structure of this debt is known with certainty. Therefore, the LqDI approach is even easier to apply in the presence of bank debt.

As with insurance companies, banks take a critical risk when they utilize an LqDI strategy. There is a chance that the withdrawal pattern they expect does not materialize, and instead that a large number of withdrawal requests come in at the same time. The bank, like the insurance company, must then start selling its Tier 2 assets quickly. If this isn't sufficient then Tier 3 assets need to be liquidated, if possible—and this is extremely costly as these are illiquid assets. If it becomes known that a bank has had a large withdrawal request and needs to liquidate many assets, especially illiquid ones, then other depositors may also put in requests to withdraw their money, worrying that the bank may run out of liquid assets. This forces the bank to liquidate even more, which may cause even more withdrawal requests. This is what is known as a "run on the bank." Bank runs are devastating due to this cascading feature of withdrawal requests and are a substantial risk that every bank has due to the mismatch of illiquid assets with a substantial part of the bank's liquid liabilities (deposits).

The bank failures in the United States in 2008 provide excellent examples of bank runs, which occur even in modern times. IndyMac, a Los Angeles-based bank that failed in the summer of 2008, was the fourth largest bank failure in the history of the United States. IndyMac had pursued an aggressive strategy of originating and investing in certain types of risky mortgages. When the mortgage market declined, beginning in 2007, the bank found itself in a vicious cycle of liquidating its investments into markets that were becoming more and more illiquid. The resulting liquidity costs caused a bank run at IndyMac. In the last week of June 2008 and the first week of July 2008, depositors withdrew $1.6 billion (about 8% of deposits). As a result, the Federal Deposit Insurance Company (FDIC) was forced to take over the bank on July 11.

The second largest bank failure in the United States took place shortly thereafter, in late September 2008. Just like IndyMac, Washington Mutual (WaMu) had a large portfolio of mortgages that yielded substantial losses when the U.S. mortgage market began declining in 2007. The losses were from the general market decline as well as liquidity costs as WaMu tried selling its mortgage holdings into an increasingly illiquid market. Eventually, a bank run occurred (beginning in mid-September 2008). Over a ten-day period, depositors pulled out $17 billion (10% of deposits). This forced the FDIC to take the bank over on September 25.

Because banks serve a critical economic function and bank runs are such a serious threat to any bank, an important mechanism has been created to help a bank potentially alleviate a bank run. The mechanism builds on the underlying idea that a bank can always try to borrow money and use these funds to meet the withdrawal requests of depositors. Essentially, the bank tries to replace one liability—

deposits—with another liability—bank borrowings. If the bank is experiencing a bank run, it is unlikely that any private lenders of any sort would be willing to lend to the troubled bank. For this reason, the Federal Reserve has been established as a so-called lender of last resort. A bank can borrow from the Federal Reserve System (the "Fed") if no other lenders are willing to lend to it. To do so, the bank has to put up some of its assets as collateral. Thus, rather than selling its assets, especially its illiquid assets, for which it would be paying substantial liquidity costs, the bank can simply borrow from the Fed up to the market value of the assets it puts up as collateral. However, this is only viable if its assets have not already experienced a substantial decrease in value due to a liquidity or market-related shock. If such a shock has already taken place, then the assets are not worth enough to cover the withdrawal requests. In such a case, borrowing from the Fed may not be enough to cover the withdrawal requests, and the bank is taken over (and its shareholders wiped out) by the bank regulators.

2.8 Liquidity Risk Exposure in Bank Balance Sheets

As we have seen, the LqDI approach is used in many types of financial institutions. As Figure 2.12 shows, this investment approach essentially matches up assets with a high degree of liquidity risk (and market risk) with long-term liabilities. The long-term nature of the liabilities mitigates the liquidity risk because the financial institution knows it will not need to liquidate those assets anytime in the near future, thus creating a return (liquidity risk premium) with low risk. Another way to think about it is that the financial institution has a long time until the liabilities come due, so it can carefully plan and time the sale of the assets so that it does not find itself in the middle of a liquidity shock as it is trying to liquidate them.

However in the case of certain financial institutions like banks and insurance companies, the long-term nature of the liabilities comes from pooling liabilities and counting on the statistical characteristic that a lot of liabilities in a pool do not come due simultaneously. Each of the liabilities nevertheless is liquid and carries very little liquidity risk. The assets that are being matched up against some of these liquid liabilities are illiquid, and carry substantial liquidity risk. As shown in Figure 2.13, this creates a "liquidity gap" between the assets and the liabilities. It is similar to the liquidity gap that we created when we constructed the liquidity premium fund earlier in this chapter.[26] The liquidity gap creates liquidity risk on the balance sheet of a bank, and this risk is borne by the shareholders, or the equity capital, of the bank.

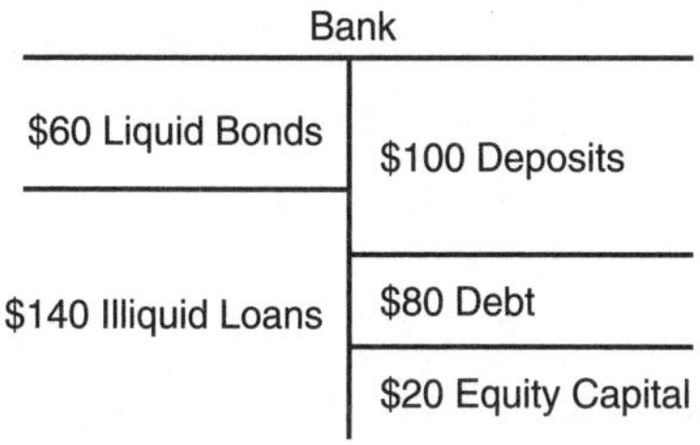

Figure 2.13   *A simple commercial bank balance sheet*

Figures 2.13 and 2.14 demonstrate how this risk manifests itself. Figure 2.13 shows a simple market value bank balance sheet with illiquid assets on the LHS and liquid liabilities on the RHS. The debt of the bank is slightly less liquid than the deposits but much more liquid than the loans on the LHS of the balance sheet. The equity capital of the bank is simply the difference between the assets and liabilities, that is, it is the amount that makes the balance sheet balance. As described earlier, a liquidity shock is a situation in which the bid curve moves down dramatically so that any investors who sell do so with substantial transaction costs. In addition, a liquidity shock is always precipitated by a sudden drop in the fundamental value of an asset (as well as a sudden increase in the volatility of the asset). The drop in the fundamental value of the asset combined with the substantial transaction costs resulting from the subsequent liquidity shock means large losses for a seller of that asset.

Bank 1	
$60 Liquid Bonds	$100 Deposits
$120 Illiquid Loans	$75 Debt
	$5 Equity Capital

Figure 2.14   *The simple bank balance sheet of Figure 2.13 after a liquidity shock*

Figure 2.14 depicts the result of a liquidity shock to the bank balance sheet in Figure 2.13 (keep in mind that these balance sheets are market value balance sheets as opposed to accounting balance sheets). When an asset is illiquid and therefore has high inherent liquidity risk, the loss of value during a liquidity shock is much greater than if the asset has low inherent liquidity risk. In Figure 2.14 therefore, when a liquidity shock hits the bank, the illiquid loans on the balance sheet decline considerably (-14%) because these assets have high liquidity risk. The bank debt also drops in value, but by much less (-6%). This is because the debt has less liquidity risk than the assets.[27] This leaves the balance sheet out of balance. To make it balance, the equity of the bank has to drop in value, which makes sense because equity is the residual claimant in any firm and therefore always takes the residual gain or loss. It is interesting to note that the equity of the bank loses 75% even though the loss on the bank's loan portfolio was a much lower percentage. This is due to the effect of leverage—the bank has a starting debt-to-asset ratio of 90%, which is a conservative leverage policy for a bank. The net effect, therefore, is that a liquidity shock causes the equity of a bank to drop in value.[28] On the other hand if liquidity experiences a positive shock, the equity capital of the bank would increase.

If we look back at Figure 2.8, which represents the return for bearing liquidity risk, an important point was made earlier that there was a steep negative return for bearing liquidity risk during the recession of 2008-2009, while there was no such negative return during the recession of 2001-2003. Putting this information together with what we just learned about the liquidity exposures of bank balance sheets, one would assume that there were substantially more bank failures during the 2008-2009 period than during the 2001-2003 period. Indeed, this turns out to be very much the case. During the 2008-2010 period more than 327 banks failed (with substantially more failures still coming as we write this in early 2011), while during the 2001-2003 period only 18 banks failed. This provides further evidence that the 2008-2009 period was a liquidity shock, while the 2001-2003 period was a conventional recession. In fact, one of the easiest ways to identify economic periods of systemic liquidity shocks is to look for periods where large numbers of financial institutions failed or were in jeopardy of failing. The last two such periods in the United States prior to 2008-2009 were the Long Term Capital Management (LTCM) crisis in 1998 and the Savings & Loan crisis in the late 1980s and early 1990s.

Banks are just one of many types of financial institutions that have liquidity gaps in their balance sheets; for example, we saw earlier that insurance companies have significant exposure to liquidity as well. In addition, we'll see later in the book that hedge funds and investment banks with capital markets and derivatives operations are also just as exposed to liquidity shocks as commercial banks.

2.9 Propagation of Liquidity Shocks: Systemic Risk

A liquidity shock always begins with a sudden decrease in the fundamental value of some asset class—quite often, as we see in subsequent chapters in the book, it is real estate. So, the question is how does a liquidity shock in one asset class propagate to other classes. The key link to this transmission is banks.

Figure 2.15 depicts a simple bank balance sheet (on a market value basis) that is facing a shift in fundamental value in one of the asset classes that it owns. Bank 1's asset structure is typical: primarily fixed income assets—some of it is relatively liquid corporate bonds, but most of it is illiquid commercial loans. The bank's liabilities consist of deposits, short-term bank borrowings from other banks, and equity capital. Notice that the debt of this bank acts as assets in the banks that lent money to this bank, Bank 2 and Bank 3 (and, in turn, Bank 2's and Bank 3's borrowings are the assets of yet other banks).

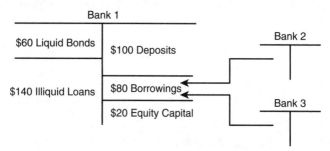

Figure 2.15 *A simple commercial bank balance sheet*

Suppose now that commercial real estate values drop. In this case, the bank's commercial real estate loans drop in value because there is a higher likelihood of default on those loans. This is the initial shock to fundamental value. The drop in fundamental value in real estate loans causes the bank's asset side of the balance sheet to shrink.

The balance sheet must balance, so the RHS of the balance sheet also shrinks, with the bank's equity taking the loss (if the bank were publicly traded, investors would see the bank's stock price drop over time as the commercial real estate loans drop in value). As a result the bank's balance sheet becomes more leveraged: Its debt-to-asset ratio (liabilities divided by assets) becomes higher. This in turn makes the loans made to the bank by other banks riskier. As these are short-term loans, the other banks may start calling these loans in.[29] In addition, some depositors, recognizing the riskier situation that the bank is in, may start withdrawing deposits. These two actions force the bank to sell some assets to come up with sufficient cash. The bank may start by trying to sell some of the real estate loans it has. However, these are typically very illiquid, and as the bank tries to sell any sizable amount of this loan portfolio the quantity structure of prices for these assets noticeably widens, with the bid curve decreasing considerably. As a result, the bank may manage to sell a small part of its real estate loans, but if it tries to sell any meaningful amount, it would accrue further losses—this time due to the sizeable liquidity costs resulting from the lower bid curve—and these losses would only exacerbate the problem the bank is facing.

The bank then is forced to move on to its next option to liquefy its balance sheet: Sell other (hopefully more liquid) assets. To this end the bank starts selling its corporate bond positions. As these are publicly traded, they are more liquid than the real estate loans. The bank reasons that selling these should allow it to raise sufficient funds without incurring huge liquidity costs. However, the corporate bonds are not perfectly liquid—they are merely more liquid than the real estate loans. As the bank starts selling the corporate bonds, the bid curve of these bonds shifts, and with most of the transactions occurring as sell transactions, the published market value of these bonds decreases.

This now creates a problem for the banks that lent to the original bank in trouble. They too are holding corporate bonds, and they see the market value of corporate bonds decrease. They are faced with a similar problem. They have had a decrease in the asset side of their balance sheets (the corporate bond positions), which results in a decrease in equity value. Furthermore, the loans they made to the original bank have also decreased in value due to the higher probability of the original bank defaulting (due to its real estate loan portfolio), which also has decreased equity value. As a result these banks become riskier and come under pressure from withdrawals and having their short-term borrowings being called back. So they too must start selling, and this is where the linkages between banks start exacerbating the situation. They start selling their corporate bond positions, which are supposed to be fairly liquid. However, with so many banks selling corporate bonds, the corporate bond market starts suffering a liquidity shock—with significant price decreases due to what are now huge liquidity costs, substantial selling, and higher volatility. What was originally a problem in commercial real estate has now spread to the corporate bond market. This major liquidity shock causes more withdrawals and more bank borrowings (at the original bank and the lending banks) to be called in. This, in turn, necessitates further liquating of all of the banks' balance sheets, so they start selling their holdings in other asset classes such as residential mortgages. The banks that have lent to the lending banks are also now facing liquidation pressure, and they are selling too.

As one can plainly see, what originally started as a simple decrease in value of commercial real estate has quickly spread from real estate to corporate bonds and then to residential mortgages and then on to other asset classes. In addition, more and more banks are getting caught up in this spiral because they have lent to each other.[30] As more banks and more asset classes get caught in what is now becoming a major financial crisis, more depositors start withdrawing funds from these banks as they hear more news about this escalating crisis. This in turn exacerbates the liquidating pressure and accelerates the crisis.

Eventually, the crisis causes the freeze-up of all financial markets as everyone is simultaneously trying to raise cash—either by selling their holdings of investable assets or withdrawing their deposits. By now, the global financial system is in the middle of a major crisis. This crisis, if it eventually spreads into the nonfinancial sector, will slow down the flow of money around the world. This slowdown of money flow will then simultaneously cause economic activity to slow down as well, because all economic activity requires money flow.

The investors and banks that have managed to monetize their holdings during the early stages of this crisis now need someplace to invest their cash. They do not want to put it into risky securities as most of these markets are in the middle of a major liquidity shock that might get even worse. Therefore, they put it into the last remaining liquid market—short-term Treasury securities. As a result, the prices of short-term Treasuries increase substantially, with a corresponding decrease in their yields.

The financial crisis in the Fall of 1998 involving Long Term Capital Management (LTCM), a prominent hedge fund, is a perfect example of how a shift in fundamental value in one small market propagated into a major worldwide liquidity shock. The precipitating event of this crisis was the default by Russia on its ruble-denominated debt. This event caused a decrease in the fundamental value of Russian bonds. LTCM's balance sheet resembled that of a bank—it had a very high debt-to-asset ratio. It started 1998 with $129 billion of assets, which was matched by $5 billion of equity and $124 billion of borrowings,[31] all of which was short-term.[32] Among its assets were Russian bonds, which had just decreased in value substantially. With very little equity capital, those banks that had lent LTCM money (which included the largest banks in the world, such as J. P. Morgan, Chase Manhattan, Deutsche Bank, Credit Suisse, Société Générale, Union Bank of Switzerland, Barclays, Goldman Sachs, Morgan Stanley, and many others) were facing the prospect of taking heavy losses on the loans they had made to LTCM and started calling in their loans. LTCM started selling its various assets to make good on these "margin calls." In addition, the various banks that had lent to LTCM started experiencing deposit withdrawals and difficulty in borrowing (or rolling over existing borrowing), thereby forcing them to sell assets as well. This propagation process continued down the chain so that lenders to the banks that had lent to LTCM were faced with liquidity pressure as well, and so on. Eventually, the bid curves in most financial markets became so low that most trading volume disappeared. Financial markets around the world froze. To avoid a complete collapse of the financial markets, the Federal Reserve Bank of New York organized a bailout of LTCM. This bailout increased the equity capital of LTCM, thereby easing concerns about losses on its loans, and therefore alleviating the need to sell assets suddenly, not only by LTCM but also all the banks in the lending chain to LTCM. Thus, bid curves throughout the financial markets returned to normal, and subsequently trading volume returned to normal.[33]

2.10 From Liquidity Crisis to Credit Crisis

What happens in the immediate aftermath of a liquidity shock? For the banks that have survived a major liquidity shock, the big problem that they face is that their equity capital has been reduced. This reduction is due to losses they have taken on their assets. The losses derive from changes in fundamental values as well as liquidity costs from selling some assets during the liquidity shock.

The reduction in banks' capital greatly increases the debt-to-asset ratio of the banks to a point where the banks are very risky; that is, the banks have very little equity to act as a buffer against any additional losses they may incur in their assets. The banks need to build back up their capital through one of two measures: earnings or raising new capital (issuing equity). Raising new equity is usually difficult to do immediately after a major liquidity shock, so banks turn their focus to profitability. However, this is a slow process, and it takes a while to build bank capital back up again.

While the banks are waiting for improved profitability to rebuild their capital, they usually take action on two important fronts to speed up this process. First they begin to sell or shut down lines of business. For example, consider the following bank balance sheet: A bank has $1 billion of assets and only $50 million in capital—the bank has a 5.0% capital ratio (capital divided by assets), which is low. To improve this ratio, the bank can shut down a line of business and sell off the assets. Suppose this bank shuts down its lending operations in a particular geographic region and sells the assets of this business for $100 million of cash. This $100 million of cash can then be used to reduce, or pay down, its liabilities by $100 million, leaving the bank with $900 million of assets and $50 million in capital. The capital ratio of the bank has now improved to 5.5%. Thus, selling off business lines accelerates the recovery in the capital ratio.

Suppose instead the bank sold the same lending business to another buyer who offered a higher amount for it: $120 million of cash. Because the business is worth only $100 million, this bid includes $20 million of profit from the sale. The $20 million of profit accrues to capital, so that the capital amount is now $70 million. Furthermore, the $120 million of cash from the sale can be used to pay down liabilities just as before, so liabilities go down to $810 million and assets go down to $880 million. The bank's capital ratio is now 8.0%. Thus, selling a business line that is highly sought after, so that the sale generates a profit, greatly accelerates the recovery of a bank's capital ratio.

The second action that banks undertake after a liquidity shock is to curtail lending to all but the highest quality borrowers. This is because of the banks' reduced debt-to-asset ratios. When a bank takes on a risky asset, it needs more capital[34] to act as a buffer against possible losses on that asset. With greatly reduced capital, banks do not have the capacity to take on risky assets such as loans to riskier borrowers. As a result it cuts down on lending, limiting loans to only the highest quality borrowers because these loans are less risky and therefore require less capital. This action lessens the amount of time the undercapitalized bank takes to rebuild its capital to a satisfactory level.

The result of these two actions by banks—shutting down of lines of business and limiting lending to only the highest quality borrowers—is an undersupply of available credit in the economy, a *credit crunch*. It is through this mechanism that liquidity shocks, which are purely financial in nature, have an effect on the nonfinancial economy; that is, how a shock to Wall Street gets transmitted to Main Street. The severity of the credit crunch depends on the severity of the liquidity crisis that preceded it and how much bank equity capital was destroyed. In the case of a severe crisis, such as the one the world went through in 2008-2009 (and, many would argue, is still ongoing as we write this in early 2011) where numerous banks failed or came close to failing, including many of the largest banks in the world,[35] the credit crunch will likely last several years.

In the following chapters, we analyze three major liquidity shocks that occurred during the 20th century and trace the shocks as they transform from a liquidity shock into a credit shock. We do so to illustrate how these liquidity shocks affect financial institutions and, subsequently, spread to the nonfinancial sector.

Endnotes

1. It is far more common to simply use the term *liquidity* rather than *transaction immediacy*, though this unfortunately creates some confusion as to the exact definition of liquidity.

2. Other commonly used terms for this cost are *bid-ask spread* and *dealer spread*.

3. Technically, a broker is not a dealer because a *dealer* is someone who will purchase an asset from a customer and hold it on its own balance sheet. A *broker*, on the other hand, is someone who merely helps or advises the owner of an asset to find another party who is willing to purchase it (or help a potential buyer of an asset to locate a seller). A broker will not purchase the asset and put it on its own balance sheet. Nevertheless, the term broker is sometimes used interchangeably with the term dealer by investors.

4. This model may be found in the article by G. Chacko, J. Jurek, and E. Stafford, "The Price of Immediacy," *Journal of Finance*, June 2008.

5. Technically, it is not merely the using up of capital on the balance sheet that is costly. The capital is invested in securities (which the dealer is holding in inventory) that earn a fair rate of return on the capital. It is the inefficiency of the use of capital that is costly. For example, holding a great deal of one security leads to a great deal of concentration, or nonsystematic, risk for which there is no risk premium. As a result, the risk is not fairly compensated and so the use of capital to hold on to this security is inefficient, and therefore costly.

6. By price volatility, we mean the volatility of the fundamental price of the security, as opposed to price volatility simply due to bouncing back and forth from the bid curve to the ask curve due to sequential sell and buy trades, or "bid-ask bounce."

7. Again, as pointed out in an earlier footnote, technically it is not the use of greater capital that results in the higher bid-ask spread but the greater inefficiency of the way the capital is being used. There is a higher opportunity cost to the dealer because the capital could be used more efficiently. It is this higher opportunity cost that is being recovered through the higher bid-ask spread.

8. This assumes that there is no trading using private information that has not yet been revealed to the markets—insider trading. If such trading existed, dealers would consistently lose to such traders, sometimes called *information traders* (in contrast to *noise traders* who trade without having private information). In this case, a dealer would have to widen its bid and ask curves to cover its losses against information traders. We do not delve into

this issue in the book because information trading in the real world is fairly small as a percentage of total market activity, and therefore securities dealers focus primarily on the costs associated with noise trading.

9. How a liquidity shock can go from individual securities to multiple securities, that is, a whole market, and then on to multiple markets is a complex process that has to do with the linkages between dealers. These linkages develop as one dealer borrows from another dealer to finance his inventory. We explain this in more detail later in the book.

10. As buys and sells are interspersed, the prices for executed buy orders coming out of a market will be much higher than the prices for executed sell orders. This is because the buy orders are being filled along the ask curve of the quantity structure of prices, while the sell orders are being filled along the bid curve. When these two curves are wide apart, as they are in a liquidity shock, the bouncing around of transactions between the bid and ask curves creates much higher volatility in the reported stream of executed transaction prices.

11. Either through revisions in the discount rate for that asset or revisions in expected future cashflows for the asset.

12. Technically, when investing in equities an investor is taking both market risk and liquidity risk in his portfolio. So this 5% number should reflect both a market risk premium and a liquidity risk premium. However liquidity risk is considered to be fairly low for most of the U.S. equity market, so that in practice all of the 5% is attributed to a market risk premium.

13. We accomplish this by only investing in bonds that are rated BBB according to Moody's credit ratings.

14. We accomplish this by investing in different bonds such that the duration of both the LHS and RHS of the balance sheet is five years.

15. We rebalance this fund every six months to ensure that the fund continues to stay neutral to default and interest rate risk.

16. It is important to note a property of liquidity here. Liquid securities tend to have low liquidity risk, while illiquid securities tend to have high liquidity risk. Essentially, if a security has low trading volume (and hence low liquidity), then any given amount of incremental selling causes a larger shift of the bid curve than if the security has high trading volume (and hence high

liquidity). The tendency of the bid or ask curves to shift due to incremental buying or selling of a security is commonly known as the *price impact* of buying or selling.

17. We will not go into the exact procedure that was used to accomplish this as it is fairly technical. The details can be found in the paper by G. Chacko and C. Evans, "Liquidity Risk in Markets," *Working Paper*, April 2010.

18. Avoiding market risk is one of the main features that hedge funds try to provide. The high fees that this industry charges in return is perhaps evidence that while avoiding market risk is feasible, it is not easy and, in fact, requires substantial skill. We discuss more about hedge funds' risk exposures later in this chapter.

19. Technically this is called *alpha* by investment professionals. Alpha refers to earning a return without taking commensurate risk. This is precisely what the investor is doing in this example—earning a liquidity premium without taking any real liquidity risk because of his long holding period for the asset.

20. In some of these funds such as private equity, even the market risk beta, and therefore the market risk premium, is high due to the leverage utilized by the funds. The liquidity risk premium then adds on to this high market risk premium.

21. Investors refer to some versions of this approach as *endowment investing*.

22. A slightly more technical definition of diverse is that customer claim events should have as close to zero correlation as possible. When one customer files a claim for a detrimental event, the probability that any other customer is also affected by the same event (and therefore also files a claim) should be near zero.

23. Technically, what insurance companies do is transfer part of the potential losses from the policies they have written to other insurance companies and investors.

24. Technically, this insurance was in the form of credit default swaps—not a conventional insurance policy. Functionally, however, a credit default swap is simply insurance for an investor against losses arising from a default.

25. The regulations are the capital adequacy requirements that banks have to follow. Banks are required to hold a certain amount of equity capital that depends on the riskiness of the investments that it makes. These rules make

it very costly for banks to invest in alternative investments because it forces banks to hold a lot of capital, thereby lowering banks' return-on-equity (ROE).

26. In fact, what we constructed in the liquidity premium fund was actually a financial institution. To test this hypothesis, we can check the correlation between the returns of the fund and the returns of a portfolio of financial institution stocks. For this portfolio, we will use the XLF exchange traded fund. The correlation between the two is 0.62—a very high value.

27. Bank debt is publicly traded and/or shorter in maturity than the loans the bank makes, and therefore, more liquid (the LqDI approach). Thus bank debt is less sensitive to changes in liquidity conditions in the markets than bank loans.

28. This is independent of any other factors because in this hypothetical example, we are holding all other factors constant. If there is also a market shock such as an interest rate shock or a commodity shock, then the respective *market* risk levels of the LHS or RHS of the balance sheet will determine the net effect of this shock on the equity capital of the bank.

29. If the terms of these loans do not allow the other banks to call them immediately, the liquidity pressure may be caused when these loans mature. At maturity the lending banks may simply choose not to roll them, that is, not extend new loans to pay off the short-term loans as they become due, thus creating liquidity pressure. This doesn't change any of the subsequent results; it simply causes them to occur a bit more slowly.

30. The risk that the failure of one bank can cause the failure of other banks because they are linked to each other due to their loans to each other is known as *systemic risk*.

31. These borrowings had many forms including short positions in various financial securities and structured products.

32. In addition it had more than $1 trillion notional of interest rate derivatives.

33. LTCM's positions were then liquidated in a more orderly fashion with limited liquidity costs after this.

34. By capital, we mean both economic capital as well as regulatory capital. If there isn't sufficient regulatory capital, a bank is not allowed to take risk. If there isn't sufficient economic capital, it is suboptimal for the bank to take risk (from the point of view of optimizing shareholder value).

35. More than 300 U.S. banks failed during 2008-2010 with more than $270 billion in assets—and this number continues to rise. However, this number does not include the number of banks that were in trouble and received government assistance. In 2009 for example, eight banks with $1.9 trillion in assets received government assistance.

chapter 3

The Great Depression

Chapter 2, "Liquidity Risk: Concepts," laid out the theoretical concept of liquidity and explained the effects of a liquidity shock on banks and financial markets. In this and the following two chapters, we turn to illustrating how these theoretical ideas manifest themselves in the actual world of financial markets and day-to-day economic activity. To do so, we focus on three historical economic crises induced by liquidity shocks—the U.S. Great Depression (1929-1933), Japan's Lost Decade (the 1990s), and the U.S. Great Recession (2007-2009).

3.1 The Stages of a Liquidity Shock

We ended Chapter 2 with a discussion on how a liquidity shock in one asset class propagates to other classes via the banking system. This systemic risk has an immediate impact on financial institutions but then subsequently can spread to the nonfinancial sector via the "credit crunch" effect that we described. Before discussing the Great Depression in this chapter, we need to go into even more detail on how a liquidity shock leads to changes in the behavior of individuals and financial institutions and to negative effects on real economic activity.

To do this, we use the flow chart in Figure 3.1 to illustrate the stages of a liquidity shock and the resulting economic downturn.

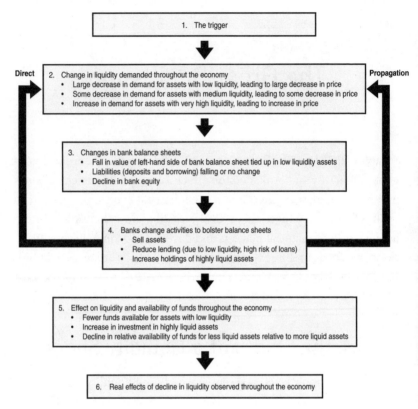

Figure 3.1 *The stages of a liquidity shock*

First, there is *an initial trigger*. Generally, this trigger is a sudden drop in the fundamental value of some asset. For example, there could be a dramatic drop in real estate prices or in the stock market.

This trigger leads to a *change in the liquidity demanded throughout the economy*. As we've discussed in previous chapters, investors become less willing to bear liquidity risk, and there is an increase in the liquidity risk premium. Investors become concerned that they will be unable to buy or sell an asset at a particular point in time at a favorable rate, and therefore turn away from assets for which that ability to buy or sell may be particularly dicey. As a classic example, consider a residential home. We are familiar with how long it may take to sell a home—from the listing, to the location of a buyer, to the working out of the conditions of the sale. In addition, the price of that home could vary tremendously depending on the broader real estate market at the time of sale. Thus, for someone who is interested in holding an asset that he or she can turn around and sell quickly at any point in time at favorable terms, a house is not an asset that would be of much interest. So, with a liquidity shock, residential real estate would be something that would become much less attractive to potential investors.

Another way to depict what a change in liquidity needs looks like is to use the most basic concepts of standard economics—supply and demand—and their relationship to price. Figure 3.2 shows the theoretical market for a highly liquid asset, such as U.S. Treasury bonds. With a liquidity shock, investors become eager to hold highly liquid assets, so the demand curve for highly liquid assets shifts from $Demand_1$ to $Demand_2$, and the *price of that highly liquid asset correspondingly jumps* from P_1 to P_2. In contrast, Figure 3.3 shows the market for an asset with very low liquidity—such as a home. Here the demand falls as investors turn away from assets with very low liquidity. Demand shifts from $Demand_A$ to $Demand_B$, and *the price of that illiquid asset correspondingly falls* from P_A to P_B.

The next stage of the liquidity shock occurs as the changes in the prices of the assets with very low liquidity hit bank balance sheets. As we discussed in Chapter 2, the change in liquidity needs throughout the economy feeds through to *changes in bank balance sheets*. Figure 3.4 again shows a prototypical bank balance sheet, along with the liquidity characteristics of the components of the balance sheet. Some of a bank's assets are highly liquid—cash and government bonds, while others are of very low liquidity, for instance loans to firms and loans to individuals. Once the liquidity shock hits and the prices of the low liquidity assets fall, there is a fall in the value of the left-hand side of the bank's balance sheet tied up in these low liquidity assets. At the same time, deposits—the main entry on the right-hand (liabilities) side of the balance sheet—might fall a bit, but by much less than the decline in assets.

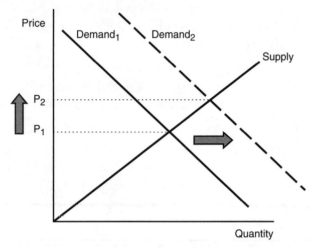

Figure 3.2   *Supply and demand for an asset with very high liquidity*

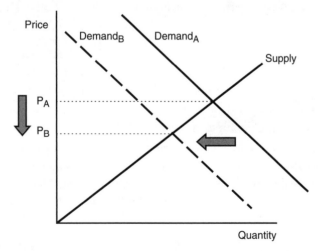

Figure 3.3   *Supply and demand for an asset with very low liquidity*

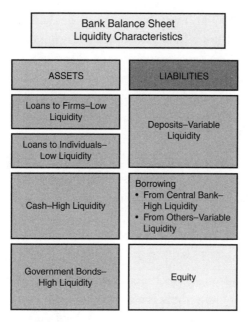

Figure 3.4   *Bank balance sheet and liquidity characteristics*

There is one more important shift in the balance sheet that occurs at this stage. On a balance sheet, both sides need to balance each other out: Assets should always equal liabilities and equity. Now, with the decline in the value of its assets (and with deposits not falling by much), a bank's equity must drop. In the case of a publicly traded bank, this would be reflected as a fall in its share price. (And as we know from our earlier discussions on bank-runs, another possibility at this point is that depositors will become nervous about the bank's riskier status and may begin to withdraw their money, which would also cause a fall in the right-hand side of the balance sheet.)

At this point, the bank faces a problem. With the decline in equity, its ratio of equity to assets—its *capital adequacy ratio*—has also fallen. The bank must therefore *change its activities to bolster its balance sheet*. It could take a number of possible actions. It could shift away from low liquidity assets by calling in loans and/or reining in new lending. It could also shift toward holding very liquid assets by investing more in cash and government bonds. Regardless, it wants to hold very liquid assets because they are safe, a key concern given the shaky capital adequacy of the bank. Moreover, given that the bank is in the midst of a liquidity shock, it also wants to hold assets with the highest liquidity possible.

It is important to remember that these changes in bank activity exacerbate the price changes in asset markets shown in Figure 3.3—a *direct feedback mechanism*. In the market for assets with very low liquidity, bank sales of these assets will lead to further declines in the prices of those assets, a downward spiral in such markets. (This is notated in Figure 3.1 by the arrow labeled "direct.")

In addition to this direct feedback loop to the market for assets with very low liquidity, there is also what we term *propagation*, notated in the diagram by another arrow. With the dramatic drop in prices in the market for assets with very low liquidity (exacerbated by the direct feedback described previously), banks that own such assets become hesitant to keep selling these assets at the now much lower price. They also don't want to drive down the price in the market for assets with very low liquidity any further. So, banks turn to selling somewhat more liquid assets to maintain sufficient internal capital. This selling leads to drops in prices in these other markets. Eventually, rounds of selling move through a wide range of markets, as banks shift from market to market searching for ways in which to take the least losses on their sales. In this way, the initial downturn in one market affects a variety of markets throughout the economy—the propagation of the liquidity shock. Another mechanism for the initial shock to be propagated is via the borrowers who have had their loans called in (revisit Figure 2.15 to see the mechanism illustrated). To meet the demands from lenders, they sell other assets that they own, further driving down prices in these other markets.

Thus far, we have focused mainly on changes in bank behavior. But these changes by banks in turn have an effect on firms and individuals throughout the economy. Initially, this effect is manifested as *fewer funds being available for assets with low liquidity and an increase in investment in highly liquid assets*. These trends may be visible in the form of changes in the terms for lending for low liquidity assets and increases in the prices of high liquidity assets.

Finally, the *real effects of the decline in liquidity hit the broader economy*—or to reuse a popular phrase: The shock moves from Wall Street to Main Street. This stage may be observed via the economic indicators commonly reported in the popular press—GDP, unemployment, housing starts, and so on.

We refer to these stages and use this framework as we work through each of the historical examples that we discuss.

3.2 Recognizing a Liquidity Shock— Interpreting the Data

Now that we know the theoretical stages of a liquidity shock, the challenge becomes finding real, measurable indicators in the data that show us how and whether a particular economic crisis is related to liquidity. In this section, we set out how we do so for the case of the U.S. Great Depression. We will then do the same in each of our subsequent historical chapters.

For any liquidity-shock induced crisis, some event or combination of events kicks off the subsequent changes in liquidity needs throughout the economy. We call it a trigger (see Table 3.1). In the case of the Great Depression, the trigger was a series of crashes in several markets: the stock market, the real estate market, and the world agricultural market. When looking for indicators for the stock market crash, we provide information on the S&P Composite Index, which tracks the stock prices of a basket of companies from a range of industries. (This measure is currently called the S&P 500,[1] as it includes 500 companies; historically, however, the number of companies included was not always 500.)[2] It provides a broader measure of the level of the stock market than the commonly used Dow Jones Industrial Average. We also consider changes in home prices for the real estate market, and, because a worldwide downturn in agriculture played an important role in this episode, we also discuss this event.

Table 3.1   *The Trigger*

Topic	Evidence
Stock market crash	S&P Composite Index
Real estate market crash	Nominal home price index
Agricultural downturn	Worldwide agricultural prices

As for the next stage, as discussed previously and illustrated in Figures 3.2 and 3.3, we look to the prices of assets with very high liquidity and assets with low liquidity as indicators of changes in the liquidity demanded throughout the economy (see Table 3.2). Residential real estate is an asset with very low liquidity. A home is a classic example of a very low liquidity asset because it often takes a long time to sell a home and the price of that home could vary tremendously depending on the broader real estate market at the time of sale. So we examine indices of both real and nominal home prices. These indices allow us to see changes over time from a certain base year, both with (real) and without (nominal) controlling for changes in overall prices. As a second example, we also show the average value of farms per acre. Farms also fall within the broad class of real estate and are also an asset with very low liquidity, since it is not easy to sell a farm at any given point in time at a predictable price. If our hypothesis regarding a liquidity shock is true, then we would expect the prices of these very low-liquidity assets to fall with the liquidity shock.

Table 3.2   *Change in Liquidity Demanded throughout the Economy*

Topic	Evidence
Decrease in Demand for Assets with Low Liquidity → Fall in Price of Low Liquidity Assets	
Residential real estate	Real home price index
	Nominal home price index
Land prices	Average value of farms per acre
Increase in Demand for High Liquidity Assets → Increase in Price of High Liquidity Assets	
Short-term federal government debt	Yields on short-term (3 to 6 month) Treasury notes and certificates
Short-term prime corporate debt	Rates on short-term (4 to 6 month) prime commercial paper

We also consider the prices of assets with very high liquidity. Short-term Treasury notes and certificates are one such asset with very high liquidity. These notes and certificates represent borrowing by the U.S. government and are easily traded in financial markets. The reason for this is that, since they will be paid off soon anyway, others are happy to purchase them at a predictable price. We also consider short-term prime commercial paper. This instrument represents borrowing by high quality firms that is intended to be repaid in a short period of time. This asset is also readily traded in financial markets, at a fairly low liquidity premium.

The data that we examine to gauge changes in prices of these assets are information on *yields*. The yield is essentially the rate of return that an investor receives for buying a particular instrument. It moves in the opposite direction of the price of the asset. If an investor is willing to accept a low yield on an asset, it means that she intrinsically values that asset more than another asset with a higher yield. An increase in the yield is equivalent to a decline in its price, while a decrease in the yield is like a rise in its price.

For the third stage of a liquidity shock (changes in bank balance sheets), we first look at the prices of low liquidity assets that might be linked to the value of certain low-liquidity entries on the asset side of bank balance sheets (see Table 3.3). We examine changes in the housing market; if real estate prices fall, the market value of any loans that banks have made in this area also fall. We also mention the decline in stock prices. Because banks made loans to borrowers for the purchase of securities, the steep fall in stock prices likely affected the value of these loans also. In addition, we look directly at some of the main categories of bank balance sheets—assets with low liquidity (loans), banks' main liability (deposits), and the value of a bank's equity (bank capital). If our hypothesis is correct, we would expect to see a decline in the value of banks' low liquidity assets, little to no change in bank deposits, and a fall in bank capital accounts. Finally, we look at overall indicators of the status of the banking sector—the number of existing banks and the number of bank suspensions. As mentioned in Chapter 2, if depositors recognize a bank's riskier situation, they might start withdrawing deposits, which could spiral into a bank run and a bank failure.

Table 3.3   *Changes in Bank Balance Sheets*

Topic	Evidence
Bursting of Asset Price Bubbles	
Stock market indicator	S&P Composite Index
Housing price indicator	Nominal and Real Housing Price Indices
Fall in Value of Bank Assets with Low Liquidity	
Bank loans	Total loans of all banks in the United States
Bank Deposits Falling or No Change	
Bank deposits	Total deposits of all banks in the United States

Topic	Evidence
Decline in Bank Equity	
Bank equity	Capital accounts of all banks in the United States
Overall Bank Viability	
Bank numbers and suspensions	Number of commercial banks in the United States
	Suspensions of commercial banks in the United States

Moving into the fourth stage of the liquidity event, as we discussed earlier, both in this chapter and in Chapter 2, banks that face a decline in the value of low liquidity assets must act to shore up balance sheets (see Table 3.4). One effective action could be to shift away from low liquidity assets, and we look to data on bank holdings of low liquidity assets to see whether they decline. For the case of the Great Depression, we examine data on the value of total loans by all commercial banks in the United States. We also look at information on the specific types of loans made by all banks that were members of the Federal Reserve System. Although this group did not include all banks in the country, these members included the more important U.S. banks and comprised about 76% of total U.S. bank resources in 1929.[3] In addition, banks at that time—and today as well, for that matter—had close relationships with each other, and most nonmember banks had deposits at member banks. Thus, the activities of the member banks provide a good indication of the activities of the overall banking sector. This information on member banks that we use is particularly interesting because it lets us see whether banks are focusing reductions in lending in areas of assets with particularly low liquidity, such as real estate and commercial loans.

We also look to bank holdings of assets with very high liquidity. Here, we focus on cash, the most liquid of assets, and also on government securities, also very liquid because they are easy to sell at a predictable price at any point in time.

Table 3.4   *Banks Change Activities to Bolster Balance Sheet*

Topic	Evidence
Reduce Lending and/or Sell Assets with Low Liquidity	
Holdings of assets with relatively low liquidity	Value of total loans by commercial banks
Holdings of assets with very low liquidity	Loans for real estate, securities, and commercial loans by all private banks that are members of the Federal Reserve System
Increase in Holdings of Assets with High Liquidity	
Holdings of assets with very high liquidity	Value of cash holdings of commercial banks
	Value of government securities holdings of commercial banks

As noted above, the changes in bank behavior induced by the liquidity shock in turn impact the availability of funds throughout the economy. (This is Stage 5—see Table 3.5.) We would expect fewer funds to be available for assets with low liquidity. To see whether this was true during the Great Depression, we examine information on residential mortgages—an asset with low liquidity at that time—looking at numbers on new mortgages, as well as at numbers on foreclosures. We also look at credit refusal or restriction experienced by the corporate sector, since commercial loans are also relatively illiquid, and we may get some information by looking at reasons why some loan requests were turned down. We examine the availability of funds to illiquid relative to more liquid assets by comparing the credit experience of small to that of large firms. Finally, as an indicator of overall credit availability we consider overall net public and private debt.

Table 3.5   *Effect on Liquidity and Availability of Funds throughout the Economy*

Topic	Evidence
General Decline in Availability of Funds for Assets with Low Liquidity	
Availability of new residential mortgages	New mortgages on 1- to 4-family houses
Status of existing mortgages	Nonfarm real estate foreclosures
Availability of funds to corporate sector	Reasons for loan refusal from survey of corporate sector
Decline in Relative Availability of Funds for Less Liquid Assets Relative to More Liquid Assets	
Availability of funds to corporate sector—small versus large firms	Credit refusal or restriction for small versus large firms from survey of corporate sector
Availability of Credit to Overall Economy	
General availability of credit	Net public and private debt

As the final stage of a liquidity shock, we expect the impact of the shrinking of credit to be felt throughout the real economy (see Table 3.6). This is when the shock moves from Wall Street to Main Street, from the financial sector to the general economy. To illustrate this stage of the crisis, we focus especially on the real estate and construction sectors. These are two sectors that generally require credit to function but that need this credit for assets (building, homes, and so on) with relatively low liquidity. The number of new housing starts and the value of new building permits tell us about whether new activity is being undertaken and/or planned, something which would require financing to get started. We also look directly at expenditures for and the value of new construction, which tell us both about the robustness of the construction sector and about the scale of new activity taking place. To learn about the state of the broader economy, we consider Gross Domestic Product (GDP), industrial production, and unemployment. GDP is the broadest measure of all of the economic

71

activity taking place in a country, while the unemployment rate tells us about jobs. Another indicator of the overall level of economic activity is the Federal Reserve's Industrial Production (IP) index; this index measures the level of activity in manufacturing, mining, and electric and gas utilities. It is an index set to a common base year, so that any possibly misleading price changes do not affect the number. We also examine price trends by taking a look at trends in both wholesale and consumer prices. All these measures, taken together, provide a good idea of the overall level of economic activity in the country after the liquidity shock hit.

Table 3.6 *Real Effects of Decline in Liquidity Observed Throughout the Economy*

Topic	Evidence
Decline in Activity in Sectors Requiring Funding but Considered to Have Relatively Low Liquidity	
Activity in real estate and construction	New housing starts
	Value of new building permits
	Expenditures for new construction
	Value of new construction put in place
Overall Economic Activity	
Gross Domestic Product (GDP)	Real GDP
Industrial Production	Industrial Production Index
Employment and Unemployment	
Unemployment rate	Unemployment rate
Overall Price Trends	
Inflation and Deflation	Wholesale Price Index
	Consumer Price Index

3.3 Setting the Stage for the Trigger— the Background for the Great Depression

Like many other recessions, the Great Depression was preceded by a period of economic boom. Industrial activity expanded dramatically during the 1920s. As discussed previously, the Federal Reserve's Industrial Production (IP) index provides a good indication of the level of overall economic activity, as it measures the level of activity in manufacturing, mining, and electric and gas utilities. Figure 3.5 shows the growth in this index, which is set to a common base year, during the period before the Great Depression. As shown, economic activity more than doubled between March 1921 and July 1929.

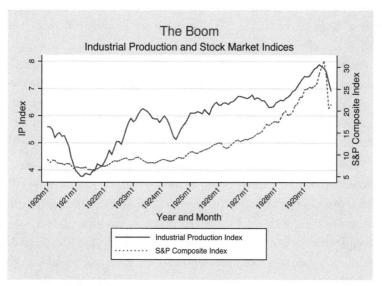

Source: Board of Governors of the Federal Reserve and Robert Shiller (http://www.econ.yale.edu/~shiller/data.htm)

Figure 3.5 *The boom*

An important part of the boom during the 1920s was growth in the automotive sector, as well as in electrical appliances, which had only recently been introduced. One factor that made such purchases affordable was the introduction of installment credit—a way in which consumers could spread out payments for a product over a longer period of time.[4] For example, the General Motors Acceptance Corporation (GMAC) started making credit for car purchases available in 1919, and total installment credit outstanding grew from $1.4 billion in 1925 to $3 billion in 1929.[5]

Another important signal of the times preceding the Great Depression comes from growth in the stock market. Figure 3.5 shows the S&P Composite Index between 1920 and 1929. The S&P Composite Index tracks the stock prices of a basket of companies from a range of industries. (This measure is currently called the S&P 500, as it includes 500 companies; historically, however, the number of companies included was not always 500.)[6] It provides a broader measure of the level of the stock market than the commonly used Dow Jones Industrial Average. It shows that the stock market grew dramatically during this decade, with much of the growth coming in 1928 and 1929, the last two years before the depression hit.

There is some debate about whether this period represented a time of "excessive" growth. Some analysts have argued that in fact this period was not one of undue pressure on resources.[7] For example, the Consumer Price Index (CPI) held relatively steady after 1923 through the end of the decade. Others, however, have suggested that excessive credit and monetary looseness led to speculation, particularly in the stock market.[8] One author of that time wrote, "The economy becomes a sick patient, sent off on a debauch, maintained on bootleg supplies, from which he will not recover for some time."[9] As one piece of information supporting this view, and again referring to Figure 3.5, U.S. stock market growth prior to 1925 generally did not exceed growth in the industrial production index. From 1925 to 1929, however, there was a distinct decoupling between the growth in stock prices and that in the Industrial Production Index. In the five-year period between September 1925 and September 1929, the S&P Composite Index grew by 240%, while the IP index only grew by 40%.

In addition to the expansion of consumer installment credit, other financial innovations of the time also likely played a role in generating the boom.[10] As one example, an *investment trust* is a way in which a group of smaller investors can join their funds to buy a more diversified set of stocks than they would be able to buy on their own.[11] Since together they have a larger total amount than each would on her own, the trust could buy, say, shares in 500 companies, as opposed to shares in 100 companies. This broader portfolio allowed the investors to be less vulnerable to changes in any one of the individual stocks that they were holding. However, these investment trusts may have fueled excessive speculation with their use of margin buying. Basically, an investment trust would borrow money to add to the contributions of each of the individuals and then use the total pool to buy stocks. With this borrowing, any declines in the value of the portfolio held by the trust meant that any losses represented an even bigger part of an individual investor's initial investment, since he now faced not only the declines in the value of the stocks purchased with the initial investment, but also the declines on the value of the stocks purchased with the money that had been borrowed to add to the pool. While the stock market was booming, however, the additional leverage often rewarded investors well.[12]

This margin buying in the stock market also contributed to the bubble.[13] At that time, investors could purchase shares with only 20¢ down on $1.00 worth of stock. The remaining 80¢ would be borrowed from brokers. The shares that they purchased using the borrowed money would be used to secure the loan being used to purchase the stock.[14] This type of loan is called a *margin loan*, and buying stock in this fashion is called *margin buying*.

With the market rising strongly, returns from dividends alone were sufficient to cover the interest that an investor owed on the margin loans, and this strategy rewarded investors well, since they enjoyed the gains from the increase in the price of stocks purchased with the borrowed money. This led investors to demand even more credit to keep taking advantage of the rising market.[15] The influx of new capital into the market further stimulated market speculation, completing the feedback loop that caused a bubble to form.

In addition to the bubble in the stock market, there was also a boom in real estate. Figure 3.6 shows construction activity between 1915 and 1930. Clearly, this sector experienced tremendous growth during the first half of the 1920s. The number of new housing starts skyrocketed from 118,000 in 1918 to 937,000 in 1925 (right axis). As shown in Figure 3.7, prices also climbed through 1925. As with the stock market, the real estate boom was fueled by borrowing. Figure 3.8 shows mortgages on one- to four-family houses, which grew substantially between 1925 and 1928. Figure 3.8 also shows overall loans by commercial banks for real estate. Here, we also see tremendous growth throughout the 1920s, indicating the increasing exposure of the commercial banking sector to changes in the real estate market.

At the time, Federal Reserve officials were concerned about signs of excessive credit in the economy. In the last six months of 1927, total bank loans and investments rose more than 3½%. There had also been rapid increases in stock prices and in brokers' loans, which are loans to brokers used to buy stocks. As discussed by Chandler (1971), at a meeting in January 1928, the resolutions of the Open Market Investment Committee (OMIC) of the Federal Reserve included the following statement: "The Committee program should now work towards somewhat firmer money conditions as far as necessary to check unduly rapid further increases in the volume of credit."[16] Indeed, the Fed began to tighten monetary policy in 1928, in part to curb the use of credit for speculation in stocks.[17]

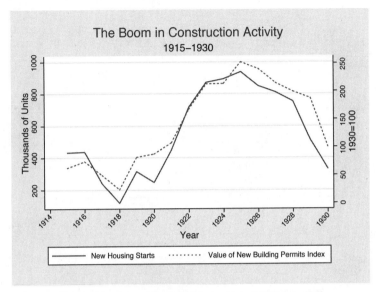

Source: *Historical Statistics of the United States, Colonial Times to 1970*
Figure 3.6 *The boom in construction*

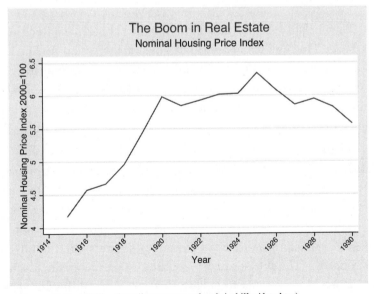

Source: Robert Shiller (http://www.econ.yale.edu/~shiller/data.htm)
Figure 3.7 *The boom in real estate*

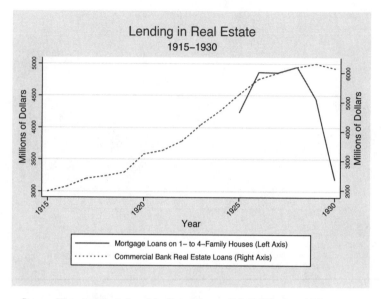

Source: *Historical Statistics of the United States, Colonial Times to 1970*
Figure 3.8 *Real estate lending*

Then in late 1929, the data show that the bubble in the stock market burst. The S&P Composite Index mentioned earlier declined by 34% between September 1929 and November 1929. Similarly, the real estate market began to fall off, beginning even earlier—starting around 1925. As an additional shock, there was a worldwide decline in commodity prices, a change that hit the agricultural sector hard.

A prolonged period of economic contraction soon followed. The debate on the exact causes of both the stock crash and the depression remains open. However, the increase in interest rates associated with the monetary tightening mentioned previously was felt throughout the economy. The Fed in fact expressed concern about this potential effect. A memo prepared for the Open Market Committee on July 17, 1928 noted, "The present high rates are testing the credit situation and it seems reasonable to believe that pressure will be felt at the weakest point, whether this is the prices of industrial securities, the volume of new issues, the amount of new building, or whatever else…"[18] The crash itself also affected the portfolio values of stock holders, leading to a sudden down-step in their net wealth and contributing to a decline in aggregate demand.

This dramatic and sudden loss in financial value from the crashes in the stock and real estate markets kicked off a period of prolonged economic hardship in the United States. A global downturn in agriculture also contributed. This era is what is called the Great Depression, and, according to the National Bureau for Economic Research (NBER), which is the body responsible for placing official dates on U.S. recessions, it lasted from August 1929 through March 1933.

In the next sections, we place this era in our framework of a liquidity crisis, showing why we believe that this historic example provides a perfect illustration of a recession induced by a shock to liquidity in the economy. Our discussion follows the phases that we described at the beginning of the chapter. We first note the triggering event (1), then changes in the liquidity demanded throughout the economy (2), changes in bank balance sheets (3), changes in bank activity (4), the effect on liquidity and availability of funds throughout the economy (5), and finally, the real effects of the decline in liquidity as observed throughout the economy (6).

3.4 Stage 1: The Trigger

For the Great Depression, a confluence of factors constituted the trigger. However, the key reason why this particular confluence had such a dramatic effect is the fact that during the 1920s banks had shifted the composition of their activities in ways that made them particularly vulnerable to the shocks to come.

Traditionally, U.S. banks focused on commercial lending. During the 1920s, however, firms (banks' traditional borrowers) began to shift to issuing securities in the capital markets and using their own internal corporate funds rather than borrowing from banks. Thus, banks increasingly shifted their asset portfolios to lending on securities and on real estate. Of note, these loans on securities were not only in the form of loans to brokers by New York banks. Rather, loans were also made to individuals on securities. So, just as real estate and securities were in the midst of the upside of bubbles, banks were shifting their lending portfolios into these sectors. For example, of the total loans and investments of all incorporated U.S. banks, the share to commercial loans fell from 47% in 1922 to 33% in 1929. At the same time, the portion going to loans on real estate rose from 9% in 1922 to 18% in 1929. For loans on securities, the change was from 13% to 20%.[19] Thus, banks became increasingly vulnerable to changes in the real estate and securities markets.

Another important characteristic of the banking sector at that time was a wide variety of interrelationships among banks in the United States. A piece published in 1932 noted, "the small country or city bank maintains an account with a neighboring city bank, or with a distant city bank, or with both."[20] In testimony before the House Committee on Banking and Currency at that time, a representative of a bank in New York estimated that it had around 3,000 other banks with which it had a correspondent relationship.[21] As was discussed in Chapter 2, this set of interrelationships would contribute to the propagation of a liquidity shock throughout the financial system.

In 1929, the value of the stock market fell sharply (see Figure 3.9). The value of housing and farms also declined. These plummets in stocks and in real estate had a heavy impact on bank assets, given the shift in bank activities that had preceded the plunge. The effects were not confined to banks in the cities; country banks had also increased their exposures in real estate and securities. To add to that, country banks had a higher exposure to farm loans than their city counterparts,[22] making them even more vulnerable to the worldwide decline in agricultural prices. In that regard, the price of wheat fell from $1.05 per bushel in 1929 to 67¢ per bushel in 1930; cotton prices also fell.[23] Of note, agriculture was an important part of the U.S. economy at the time of the Great Depression. In 1929, about 25% of total employment in the United States was in agriculture. In fact, President Herbert Hoover in his December 1930 State of the Union address placed some blame for the Great Depression on excess production worldwide in "wheat, rubber, coffee, sugar, silver, zinc and to some extent cotton."[24]

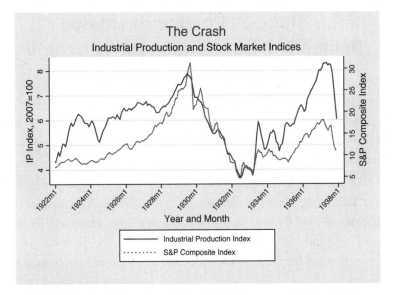

Source: Board of Governors of the Federal Reserve and Robert Shiller (http://www.econ.yale.edu/~shiller/data.htm)

Figure 3.9 *The stock market crash*

The nature of finance within the stock market, as discussed previously, exacerbated these effects. Given the high level of borrowing that had been associated with stock purchases—"margin buying"—the steep fall in share values meant that all those who were heavily levered (i.e., those who had taken out loans to buy stocks, using the stocks as collateral) would have their loans called in. They in turn would need to liquidate their positions; that is, sell the stocks that they owned. This selling in turn led to a downward spiral in the stock market. Moreover, investors likely faced the need to liquidate other available assets, pushing prices in other asset markets down as well.

As a final point, the Federal Reserve's tightening of monetary policy beginning in 1928 also had broader effects on aggregate demand, providing additional dampening to economic activity.

3.5 Stage 2: Change in Liquidity Demanded Throughout the Economy

This confluence of adverse shocks led to a *change in liquidity demanded throughout the economy*. Broadly speaking, there was an increase in demand for high-liquidity assets and a decline in demand for low liquidity assets. This increase was reflected in asset prices and financial markets during this era.

As one indicator, Figure 3.10 provides real and nominal housing price indices for this time period. The nominal index is an indicator of the price level of homes, while the real index eliminates the effects of overall changes in prices. As shown, both real and nominal home prices plunged from about 1928 through 1933. Given that homes are a relatively illiquid asset, this direction of change is consistent with a decline in the price of assets with low liquidity. It is also suggestive of the effects on the balance sheets of banks holding mortgages on their books. Another relatively illiquid asset, farms, experienced a similar plunge in prices. Figure 3.11 shows that the average value of farms per acre fell dramatically between 1930 and 1933. Of course, this fall also reflects the worldwide agricultural downturn mentioned earlier.

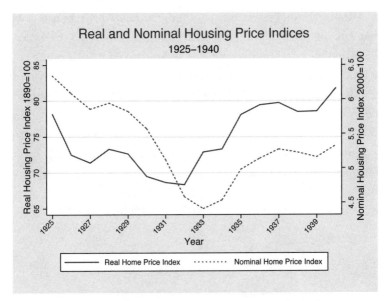

Source: Robert Shiller (http://www.econ.yale.edu/~shiller/data.htm)

Figure 3.10   *Housing prices*

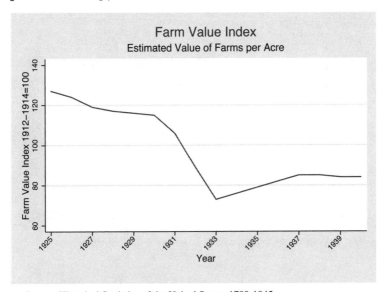

Source: Historical Statistics of the United States, 1789-1945

Figure 3.11   *Farm value index*

Other data suggest an increase in the absolute price of assets with relatively high liquidity. Figure 3.12 shows the yield on 3- to 6-month U.S. Treasury notes and certificates and on 4-to 6-month prime commercial paper. As noted earlier, both of these instruments represent short-term loans—to the U.S. government in the case of the treasuries and to low-risk firms in the case of the prime commercial paper. Since such short-term loans will come due soon anyway, they are easily sold to others at predictable prices. Figure 3.12 shows that both experienced a dramatic decline in yields (which move in the opposite direction of prices) starting in 1929. Again, this movement is consistent with an increased value being placed on assets with high liquidity.

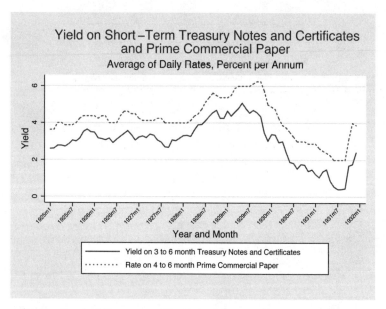

Source: Board of Governors of the Federal Reserve, Banking and Monetary Statistics

Figure 3.12 *Short-term loans to U.S. government and to corporations*

3.6 Stage 3: Changes in Bank Balance Sheets

As a first indicator of possible changes in bank balance sheets, we refer back to Figures 3.9 and 3.10, which show the steep declines in housing and stock prices. This provides our first suggestion as to possible changes in the balance sheets of banks holding loans backed by such assets on their books. We can also examine the broad categories of assets and liabilities on bank balance sheets. If our hypothesis is correct, we would expect to see a decline in the value of banks' low liquidity assets, little to no change in bank deposits, and a fall in bank capital. Indeed, as shown in Figure 3.13, total loans by all banks in the United States plunged after 1929. The value of these total loans fell by just more than 50%—$22 billion—between 1929 and 1935. At the same time, the right-hand side of the balance sheet should fall a bit, but by less than the decline in assets. For the case of the Great Depression, total deposits fell by 12%—about $7 billion—during 1929 and 1935. We had also suggested that bank equity would fall. As shown in Figure 3.13, it did indeed decline—by 20% or $2 billion between 1929 and 1935.

We also look at overall indicators of the status of the banking sector. For one, given the possibility of depositor fears about bank viability, we might observe people withdrawing deposits, which could spiral into a bank run and a bank failure. Deposits did decline, as we discussed previously and show in Figure 3.13. In addition, as shown in Figure 3.14, bank suspensions skyrocketed beginning in 1930, while the number of banks in operation plunged.

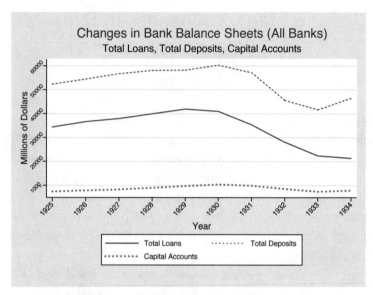

Source: *Historical Statistics of the United States, Colonial Times to 1970*
Figure 3.13   *Changes in bank balance sheets*

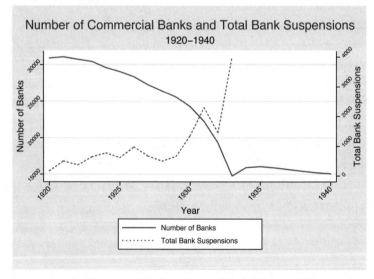

Source: *Historical Statistics of the United States, Colonial Times to 1970*
Annual data for bank suspensions and deposits from suspended banks not provided after 19:
Figure 3.14   *Bank failures*

3.7 Stage 4: Banks Change Activities to Bolster Balance Sheets

Faced with changes in its balance sheet, such as a decline in the value of low liquidity assets, a bank must take action to shore up the balance sheet. One effective action could be to shift away from low liquidity assets. Such a change in behavior indeed appears to have occurred during the Great Depression. Figure 3.15 shows assets for all commercial banks in the United States. Starting in 1929, the value of bank loans began to shrink. At the same time, holdings of cash and U.S. government debt instruments were fairly flat or increased slightly. This change is consistent with a financial institution choosing to shift its assets into higher liquidity investments.

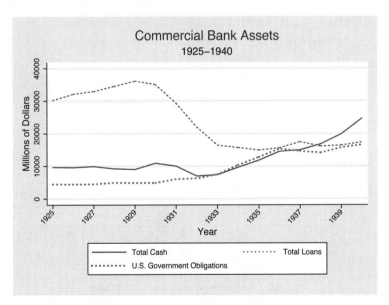

Source: *Historical Statistics of the United States, Colonial Times to 1970*
Figure 3.15 *Commercial bank assets*

Figure 3.16 provides more details on bank assets over a shorter period of time, October 1929 through June 1932. These numbers are for banks that were members of the Federal Reserve System, a group that included the more important U.S. banks and comprised about 76% of total U.S. bank resources in 1929.[25] These banks also had close relationships with nonmember banks, so the activities of the member banks should provide a good indication of the activities of the overall banking sector. Figure 3.16 is set up so that all of the loan categories are equal to 100 in June 1929. Each of the lines then shows the changes in each category over this time period. Here, it is clear that the decline in lending came mainly via falls in commercial loans and loans on securities— both assets with low liquidity. On the other hand, investment in government bonds, both federal and local, rose substantially. This movement into government bonds is not surprising; with a decline in its capital base, a bank could ill afford to take risks with its investments. Funds needed to be kept in the most liquid and safest location possible.

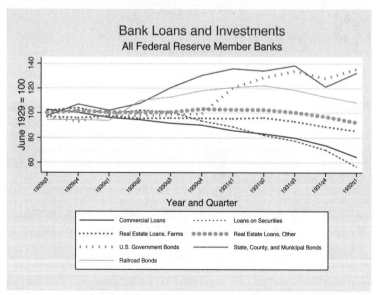

Source: National Industrial Conference Board (1932), Federal Reserve Board
Figure 3.16 *Fed member bank assets by type*

At this point, we'd also like to get an idea of what banks were doing with new funds coming in. Figure 3.17 shows commercial bank liabilities and capital, the right-hand side of the bank balance sheet, over a longer period of time. Total deposits initially fell starting in 1929; in terms of the bank balance sheet, this implies that lending would need to be constrained. However, deposits began to bounce back in 1933. Loans, on the other hand, did not turn up until three years later—in 1936 (as shown in Figure 3.15), and then only slightly. Banks, rather than loaning out the increased deposits apparently instead used these funds in other ways, such as investing in safe and highly liquid assets. Indeed, returning again to Figure 3.15, beginning in 1933, we see sizeable increases in bank investment in both U.S. government obligations and cash.

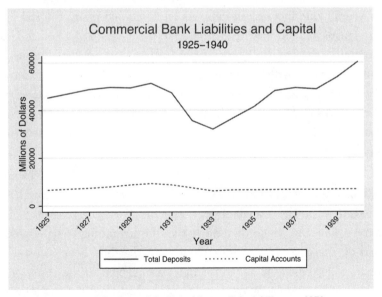

Source: *Historical Statistics of the United States, Colonial Times to 1970*
Figure 3.17   *Commercial bank liabilities*

3.8 Stage 5: Effect on Liquidity and Availability of Credit Throughout the Economy

Earlier, we suggested that these changes by banks would in turn have an effect on firms and individuals throughout the economy, with fewer funds being available for assets with low liquidity and an increase in investment in highly liquid assets. The slowdown in lending indeed had a dramatic effect on the availability of credit during the Great Depression. For one, as shown in Figure 3.18, there was a sizeable decline in mortgage loans on one- to four- family houses. Recalling the boom in real estate that we discussed earlier, this drop represented a sizeable shrinkage from the real estate expansion fueled in earlier years by an increase in debt. As an additional point, the spike in mortgages in 1933 may be attributed to the creation of a new federal program—the Home Owners' Loan Corporation—designed to assist families dealing with potential home foreclosures.[26] Figure 3.19 shows the number of foreclosures on nonfarm real estate. The steep increase through 1933 suggests the state of borrowing in real estate: many loans were being called in and borrowers were losing the assets that they had borrowed to purchase.

An interesting survey of industrial concerns conducted by the National Industrial Conference Board in August and September 1932 sheds light on the availability of credit to the corporate sector. This survey aimed to gauge the effects that the tightening of bank credit had on the corporate sector. When firms that had been refused or restricted credit were asked for the reasons, 66% of the cases were due to either the condition or policy of the bank, not the condition of the firm applying for credit. In addition, the survey found that recent reductions in bank credit had fallen disproportionately on small firms.[27] Given that these loans would tend to be the least liquid of all corporate lending, it is consistent with our overall hypothesis.

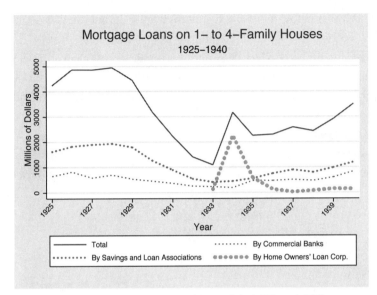

Source: *Historical Statistics of the United States, Colonial Times to 1970*
Figure 3.18   *Mortgage loans*

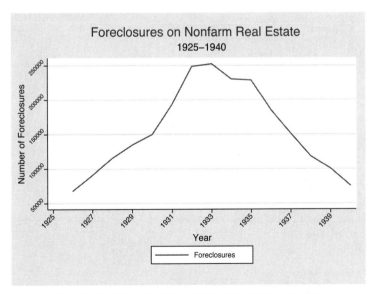

Source: *Historical Statistics of the United States, Colonial Times to 1970*
Figure 3.19   *Foreclosures*

Most broadly, there was a general decline in net debt throughout the economy. Figure 3.20 shows net public and private debt. Beginning in the early 1930s, both corporate and noncorporate/individual net debt began to decline. After 1933, it remained subdued through the remainder of the decade. Federal debt, on the other hand, picked up after President Franklin D. Roosevelt took office in March 1933. All told, our evidence suggests that the Great Depression provides a perfect example of the potential effects of a liquidity shock on the availability of credit throughout the economy.

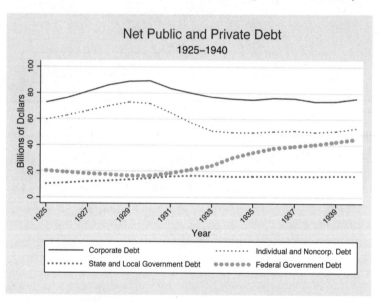

Source: *Historical Statistics of the United States, Colonial Times to 1970*

Figure 3.20   *Broad debt*

3.9 Stage 6: Real Effects of Decline in Liquidity Observed Throughout the Economy

As the final stage of a liquidity shock, we expect the impact of the shrinking of credit to be felt throughout the real economy; or, to use a phrase that we mentioned previously, the shock moves "from Wall Street to Main Street." To illustrate this stage of the crisis, we focus especially on real estate and construction—sectors that generally require credit to function but that need this credit for assets (building, homes, etc.) with relatively low liquidity. Figure 3.21 provides the number of new housing starts (left axis) and an index of the value of new building permits issued (right axis). These both give us a gauge of the level of new activity starting up in the real estate sector. Both indicators show marked downturns through 1934.

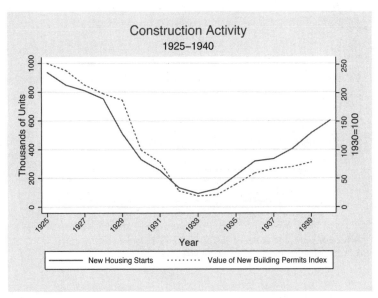

Source: *Historical Statistics of the United States, Colonial Times to 1970*

Figure 3.21 *Construction activity*

We also look directly at expenditures for and the value of new construction, which tell us both about the robustness of the construction sector and about the scale of new activity taking place. These trends also suggest an overall slowing of activity. Figure 3.22 provides expenditures on private residential, private nonresidential, and public new construction. The private numbers fell beginning in the late 1920s, as the real estate bubble burst. They remained subdued through 1934. This reduction in expenditures on new construction of course affected the value of new construction put in place—shown in Figure 3.23. To the extent that these numbers imply a decline in a country's infrastructure, this may be one mechanism via which a liquidity crisis could have long-lasting, real effects.

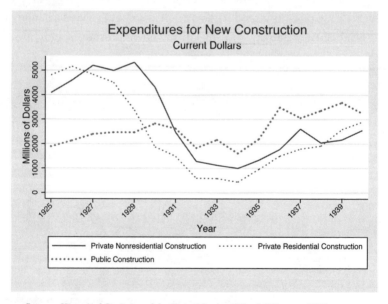

Source: *Historical Statistics of the United States, Colonial Times to 1970*
Figure 3.22 *Expenditures for new construction*

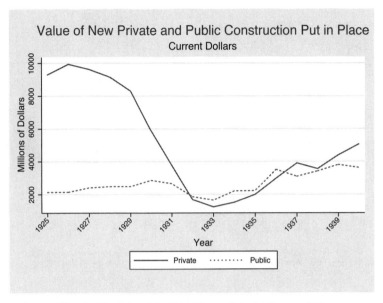

Source: *Historical Statistics of the United States, Colonial Times to 1970*
Figure 3.23 *Value of new construction put in place*

More information about the overall economy at that time is provided by trends in prices. Figure 3.24 shows the Wholesale Price Index (WPI) and the Consumer Price Index (CPI). The WPI provides an indication of the overall level of prices faced by producers, while the CPI shows the overall level of prices faced by consumers. An increase in either indicates rising prices—inflation—while a decrease indicates falling prices—deflation. As shown, prices plunged beginning in 1929/30 and did not begin to reverse until 1933. These general declines in prices would also have an effect on bank balance sheets. Generally, deflation makes it harder for a borrower to pay back a loan. Thus, any concerns about bank solvency may be exacerbated by an overall deflationary environment.

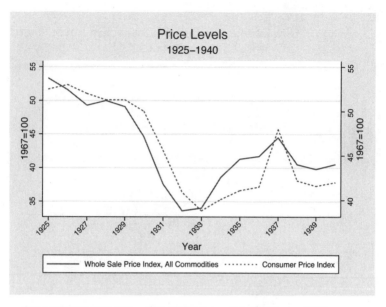

Source: *Historical Statistics of the United States, Colonial Times to 1970*
Figure 3.24   *Prices*

Finally, Figure 3.25 provides two broad indicators of the state of the economy—real GDP and unemployment—that reflect the extent of the downturn sparked by this liquidity crisis. GDP is the broadest measure of all the economic activity taking place in a country. "Real" GDP eliminates the effects of changes in prices, so it tells us directly about the actual output of the economy. As Figure 3.25 shows, real GDP plunged beginning in 1929, and unemployment skyrocketed. Figure 3.26 provides another indicator of the overall level of economic activity—the Industrial Production (IP) index. Here also, we observe the steep decline in economic activity between 1929 and 1933. These measures, taken together, provide a good idea of the overall level of economic activity in the country after the liquidity shock hit.

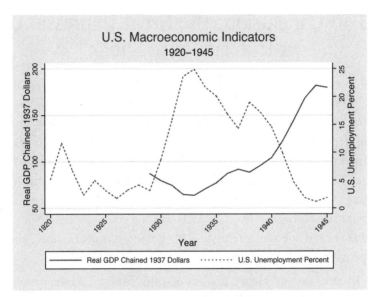

Source: U.S. Bureau of Economic Analysis, Mitchell (1993)
Figure 3.25 *GDP and unemployment*

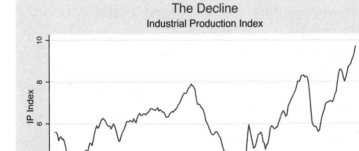

Source: Board of Governors of the Federal Reserve
Figure 3.26 *Industrial Production index*

3.10 Conclusion: The Great Depression, a True Liquidity Shock

The evidence presented in this chapter illustrates how a liquidity shock may be transmitted throughout the economy, as the banking sector shifts away from its traditional function of channeling funds from depositors to borrowers. This credit tightening in turn impacts the real sector and overall economic activity. As with the origins of the Great Depression, the reasons for its resolution remain open to debate. One common view posits that the Great Depression was ended by the advent of World War II and the corresponding increase in war-related spending. Christina D. Romer, however, places more emphasis on monetary factors.[28]

In any case, as Figure 3.27 shows, the banking sector resumed growth in lending around 1943, when an increase in deposits (see Figure 3.28) was directed into both government bonds and lending. This distribution contrasts starkly with bank behavior during the liquidity crisis when available funds were channeled out of loans and into the most liquid asset available—U.S. government bonds. Bank equity—the capital accounts shown previously in Figure 3.26—also recovered. The liquidity crisis over, banks could resume their normal role of channeling funds and taking on liquidity risk—a function that allows an economy to grow.

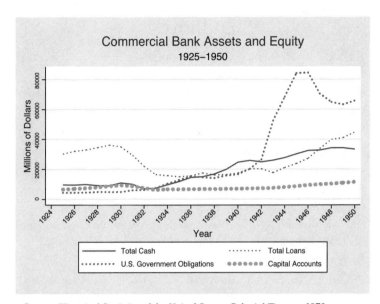

Source: *Historical Statistics of the United States, Colonial Times to 1970*
Figure 3.27 *Commercial bank assets, recovery*

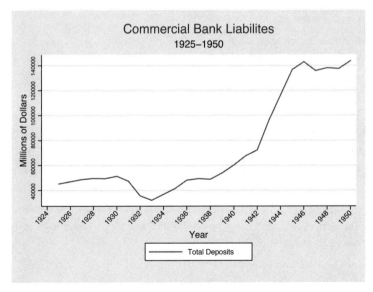

Source: *Historical Statistics of the United States, Colonial Times to 1970*
Figure 3.28 *Commercial bank deposits, recovery*

Endnotes

1. The S&P 500 is an index of the prices of large-cap common stocks actively traded in the United States and probably the best known of the many indices from the financial services company Standard & Poor's (S&P).

2. For more information about the data series that we use, see Robert S. Shiller (2006) *Irrational Exuberance*. New York: Random House.

3. National Industrial Conference Board (1932) *The Banking Situation in the United States*. New York: National Industrial Conference Board.

4. Federal Reserve Bank of Boston (2004) "The Evolution of Consumer Credit in America." *The Ledger*, Spring/Summer 2004. Available at http://www.bos.frb.org/education/ledger/ledger04/sprsum/sprsum04.pdf; Charles P. Kindleberger (1977) *The World in Depression, 1929-1939*. London: Allen Lane.

5. Federal Reserve Bank of Boston (2004) "The Evolution of Consumer Credit in America." *The Ledger*, Spring/Summer 2004. Available at http://www.bos.frb.org/education/ledger/ledger04/sprsum/sprsum04.pdf; Charles P. Kindleberger (1977) *The World in Depression, 1929-1939*. London: Allen Lane.

6. For more information about the data series that we use, see Robert S. Shiller (2006) *Irrational Exuberance*. New York: Random House.

7. For example, see Lester V. Chandler (1971) *American Monetary Policy, 1928-1941*. New York: Harper & Row; Charles P. Kindleberger (1977) *The World in Depression, 1929-1939*. London: Allen Lane.

8. Lester V. Chandler (1971) *American Monetary Policy, 1928-1941*. New York: Harper & Row, Publishers and Charles P. Kindleberger (1977) *The World in Depression, 1929-1939*. London: Allen Lane also discuss these views.

9. C. Reinold Noyes, "The Gold Inflation in the United States, 1921-1929," *American Economic Review*, June 1933, 197, as cited in Lester V. Chandler, *American Monetary Policy, 1928-1941*.

10. Jeremy Atack and Peter Passell (1994) "The great depression: explaining the contraction." *A New Economic View of American History*. New York: WW Norton. The authors provide an overall discussion of the role of

financial innovations in leading to the stock market crash in their book, on pages 604 to 607. Atack and Passell credit John Kenneth Galbraith (1972) *The Great Crash*. Boston: Houghton Mifflin as suggesting the importance of financial innovation and changes in market operations in leading to the stock market crash. The investment trust is discussed by Atack and Passell on pages 604-605, where they also mention Galbraith.

11. This next three paragraphs draw heavily from Jeremy Atack and Peter Passell (1994) "The great depression: explaining the contraction." *A New Economic View of American History*. New York: WW Norton. See page 605.

12. Jeremy Atack and Peter Passell (1994) "The great depression: explaining the contraction." *A New Economic View of American History*. New York: WW Norton. See page 605.

13. Jeremy Atack and Peter Passell (1994) "The great depression: explaining the contraction." *A New Economic View of American History*. New York: WW Norton. The authors provide an overall discussion of the role of financial innovations in leading to the stock market crash in their book, on pages 604 to 607. Atack and Passell credit John Kenneth Galbraith (1972) *The Great Crash*. Boston: Houghton Mifflin as suggesting the importance of financial innovation and changes in market operations in leading to the stock market crash. Pages 605 to 606 provide a discussion of margin buying, where the authors mention Galbraith.

14. Jeremy Atack and Peter Passell, "The great depression: explaining the contraction." *A New Economic View of American History*. New York: WW Norton provide an overall discussion of the role of financial innovations in leading to the stock market crash in their book, on pages 604 to 607. Atack and Passell credit John Kenneth Galbraith (1972) *The Great Crash*. Boston: Houghton Mifflin as suggesting the importance of financial innovation and changes in market operations in leading to the stock market crash. Pages 605 to 606 provide a discussion of how margin buying worked, where the authors mention Galbraith.

15. Jeremy Atack and Peter Passell (1994) "The great depression: explaining the contraction." *A New Economic View of American History*. New York: WW Norton. See page 605.

16. Lester V. Chandler (1971) *American Monetary Policy, 1928-1941*. New York: Harper & Row, p. 38.

17. Lester V. Chandler (1971) *American Monetary Policy, 1928-1941*. New York: Harper & Row, p. 37-46.

18. Lester V. Chandler (1971) *American Monetary Policy, 1928-1941*. New York: Harper & Row, p. 48.

19. National Industrial Conference Board (1932) *The Banking Situation in the United States*. New York: National Industrial Conference Board, p. 75.

20. National Industrial Conference Board (1932) *The Banking Situation in the United States*. New York: National Industrial Conference Board, p. 24.

21. "Hearings on Branch, Chain, and Group Banking," House Committee on Banking and Currency, 71st Congress, 2nd Session, H.R. 141, Vol. 2, Part 14, pp. 1808 and 1841 as cited in National Industrial Conference Board (1932) *The Banking Situation in the United States*. New York: National Industrial Conference Board, pp. 24-25.

22. National Industrial Conference Board (1932) *The Banking Situation in the United States*. New York: National Industrial Conference Board, p. 119.

23. Jeremy Atack and Peter Passell (1994) "The great depression: explaining the contraction." *A New Economic View of American History*. New York: WW Norton, p. 594.

24. Department of State. *Foreign Relations of the United States, 1930*. Vol. 1, Washington, DC: U.S. Government Printing Office, 1945, vii, as cited in Charles P. Kindleberger (1977) *The World in Depression, 1929-1939*. London: Allen Lane, p. 83.

25. National Industrial Conference Board (1932) *The Banking Situation in the United States*. New York: National Industrial Conference Board.

26. For more information, see *History and Policies of the Home Owners' Loan Corporation* by C. Lowell Harriss, Publisher: UMI, ISBN: 0-870-14142-2; http://www.nber.org/books/harr51-1.

27. National Industrial Conference Board (1932) *The Availability of Bank Credit*. New York: National Industrial Conference Board, pp. 74-75.

28. Christina D. Romer (1992) "What Ended the Great Depression?" *The Journal of Economic History*. Cambridge University Press. December 1992.

References

Atack, Jeremy and Peter Passell. 1994. "The great depression: explaining the contraction." *A New Economic View of American History*. New York: WW Norton.

Board of Governors of the Federal Reserve. Banking and Monetary Statistics 1914-1941: 1914-1941. http://fraser.stlouisfed.org/publications/bms/.

Board of Governors of the Federal Reserve. Banking and Monetary Statistics 1941-1970: 1941-1970. http://fraser.stlouisfed.org/publications/bms2/

Chandler, Lester V. 1971. *American Monetary Policy, 1928-1941*. New York: Harper & Row.

Department of State. *Foreign Relations of the United States, 1930*. Vol. 1, U.S. Government Printing Office, Washington, DC, 1945, vii, as cited in Kindleberger. 1977. 83.

Federal Reserve Bank of Boston. 2004. "The Evolution of Consumer Credit in America." *The Ledger*. Spring/Summer 2004, available at http://www.bos.frb.org/education/ledger/ledger04/sprsum/sprsum04.pdf.

Galbraith, John Kenneth. 1972. *The Great Crash*. Boston: Houghton Mifflin, as cited in Atack and Passell. 1994.

Harriss, C. Lowell. 1951. *History and Policies of the Home Owners' Loan Corporation*. National Bureau of Economic Research. available at http://www.nber.org/books/harr51-1.

House Committee on Banking and Currency. "Hearings on Branch, Chain, and Group Banking." 71st Congress, 2nd Session, H.R. 141,

Vol. 2, Part 14, pp. 1808 and 1841. as cited in National Industrial Conference Board. 1932. *The Banking Situation in the United States*. 25.

Kindleberger, Charles P. 1977. *The World in Depression, 1929-1939*. London: Allen Lane.

Mitchell, B. R. 1993. *International Historical Statistics: The Americas, 1750-1988*. New York: Stockton Press.

National Industrial Conference Board. 1932. *The Availability of Bank Credit*. New York: National Industrial Conference Board.

National Industrial Conference Board. 1932. *The Banking Situation in the United States*. New York: National Industrial Conference Board.

Noyes, C. Reinold. "The Gold Inflation in the United States, 1921-1929." *American Economic Review*. June 1933. 197, as cited in Chandler, *American Monetary Policy, 1928-1941*, 18.

Romer, Christina D. 1992. "What Ended the Great Depression?" *The Journal of Economic History*. Cambridge University Press.

Shiller, Robert S. 2006. *Irrational Exuberance*. Random House, Inc.

U.S. Bureau of the Census. 1949. *Historical Statistics of the United States, 1789-1945*, A Supplement to the Statistical Abstract of the United States. Washington, DC: U.S. Bureau of the Census.

U.S. Bureau of the Census. 1975. *Historical Statistics of the United States, Colonial Times to 1970*, Bicentennial Edition. Washington, DC: U.S. Bureau of the Census.

chapter 4

Japan's Lost Decade

In this chapter, we turn to illustrating another historical economic crisis: the liquidity-shock induced recession suffered by Japan during the 1990s, sometimes referred to as Japan's "Lost Decade."[1] Just as we did when we looked at the Great Depression in Chapter 3, we'll first review our general framework on how a liquidity shock leads to changes in the behavior of individuals and financial institutions and to negative effects on real economic activity, before we discuss actual events.

4.1 The Stages of a Liquidity Shock— Revisited and Expanded

The flowchart in Figure 4.1 provides a more abbreviated version of the stages of a liquidity shock and the resulting economic downturn that we discussed in Chapter 3, "The Great Depression." There is first *an initial trigger*. With the Great Depression, we observed that it was the combination of crashes in real estate, stocks, and worldwide commodity prices. For the case of Japan, we will again identify a sudden drop in the fundamental value of some asset as a trigger.

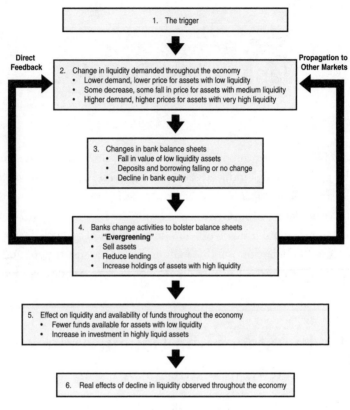

Figure 4.1 *The stages of a liquidity shock*

This trigger in turn leads to a *change in the liquidity demanded throughout the economy*. Investors become concerned that they will be unable to buy or sell an asset at a particular point in time at a favorable rate, and therefore turn away from assets that may become hard to buy or sell quickly, with a residential home being a classic example. With a liquidity shock, residential real estate becomes much less attractive to potential investors. Thus, with a liquidity shock, prices of assets with low liquidity should fall. In contrast, investors become eager to hold highly liquid assets, so the prices of highly liquid assets should rise.

The next stage of the liquidity shock manifests itself as *changes in bank balance sheets*. Once the liquidity shock hits and the prices of the low liquidity assets fall, there is a fall in the value of the left-hand side of a bank's balance sheet tied up in these low liquidity assets. The main entry on the right-hand (liabilities) side of the balance sheet—deposits—may fall a bit, but by much less than the decline in assets. At the same time, and dictated by the fact that the two sides of the balance sheet must always be equal, the decline in the value of its assets means that a bank's equity must also fall.

Subsequently, banks must *change activities to bolster their balance sheets*. With the decline in equity, the bank's ratio of equity to assets has also fallen. The bank could now shift away from low liquidity assets—by calling in loans and/or reining in new lending. It will likely also shift toward holding very liquid assets—investing more in cash and government bonds. It wants to hold very liquid assets because they are both very liquid and low risk. As we noted earlier, there are also two ways in which changes in bank activities feed back into prices in financial markets—directly and via propagation to other markets.[2]

For the case of Japan, we want to introduce one additional way in which banks may change their behavior in response to the changes in their balance sheets caused by the fall in the price of assets with low liquidity. Consider the case of a bank holding a loan to a corporate borrower that it knows is close to bankruptcy. The only way that the borrowing firm can stay open is if it gets additional money from the bank. The bank now must choose between two options: (1) It could refuse to extend additional credit to the firm, the firm would default on its loan, and the bank's assets would fall by the amount of that loan; *or* (2) the bank could give the nearly bankrupt firm another loan, the firm would remain in operation (using some of the new loan to make payments on the existing loan), and the bank would keep both the old and the new loan on its books. From the perspective of the balance sheet of a bank with an equity to assets ratio close to the required minimum, option 2 would be attractive—it could keep the loans on its books and not face additional deterioration in its capital to assets ratio.

Bank accommodation of a troubled firm could also occur in a more subtle way. Consider the case of a bank holding a troubled loan; the bank knows that the borrower is not likely to repay the loan, but the loan remains on the bank's books. Once the borrower defaults, it is clear how this would affect the bank's balance sheet—there would be a decline on the asset side in the amount of the value of the loan. Before default actually occurs, a borrower may stop making payments on the loan; after a number of missed payments, the loan may become classified as "nonperforming." Once that happens, the bank needs to create something called a *loan loss reserve*. A loan loss reserve is money that a bank sets aside just in case a borrower defaults; it reduces the amount by which assets fall if the borrower does eventually default. A loan loss reserve is a bit like insurance for a bank against future losses—it is a prudent way to reduce losses from future defaults. However, it is also costly for a bank to put money aside for a loan loss reserve. Any money that it puts into the loan loss reserve could have instead been put into bank equity. A bank that faces a low equity to assets ratio right now will want to put every yen of income into equity rather than setting it aside into loan loss reserves. Returning to the troubled loan, if the bank extends a bit more credit to the borrower, the borrower will be able to keep making payments. If payments continue, then the bank itself can avoid declaring the loan "nonperforming" and needing to set aside money in the loan loss reserve.[3]

These two behaviors—continuing to extend credit to firms likely to go bankrupt and to firms whose loans are likely to become nonperforming—have together been termed *evergreening*.[4] The loan is always living—ever green—since the bank keeps lending, despite the underlying weakness of the borrower. Evergreening helps a bank that has a shaky capital to asset ratio. It avoids the hit to assets and to the capital to assets ratio caused by a default; the practice allows the bank to direct income directly into capital, rather than into loan loss reserves. The downside, of course, is that the bank is essentially sweeping the toxic nature of its loan portfolio "under the rug." In addition, it is making future losses even larger by not building up a loan loss reserve.

Returning to our stages of a liquidity shock, we need to add ever-greening to one of the ways in which banks may change their activities in response to a liquidity shock. By using this strategy, the bank on the surface appears to be maintaining a reasonable capital to equity ratio, as well as continuing to lend. Evergreening was widely used during Japan's Lost Decade, as we describe later in this chapter.

Next (Stage 5 in Figure 4.1), we need to bring in the fact that the changes by banks affect firms and individuals throughout the economy, as *fewer funds become available for assets with low liquidity, and there is increased investment in highly liquid assets.* For the case of Japan, we need to make an additional point. The evergreening that we explained earlier—when banks roll over loans to troubled borrowers, rather than letting the borrower default and writing off the loan—has profound implications for the pattern of any lending that does take place. Since funds (and liquidity) are tied up in rollover loans, credit could be even less available for potentially worthy borrowers than would be the case without the evergreening. Furthermore, the timing of the impact of the liquidity shock may be delayed.

As the final stage of the liquidity shock, the real effects of the change in availability of funds hit the broader economy. The *real effects of the decline in liquidity will be observed throughout the economy,* which may be observed via the macroeconomic indicators commonly reported. At this point, the economy is in a recession that at its surface may appear similar to other recessions not induced by a liquidity shock. And for the case of Japan, this recession extended over a long span of time.

4.2 Recognizing a Liquidity Shock— Interpreting the Data

To show how a liquidity shock may manifest itself, we again look to real, measurable indicators in the data that show us how and whether a particular economic crisis is related to liquidity. In this section, we set out exactly how we will do so for Japan's Lost Decade.

The initial event in these liquidity-shock induced crises is a trigger (see Table 4.1). For the case of Japan, the precipitous decline in real estate prices in 1990 was a critical factor. We consider an index of prices of urban land. We have information on urban land prices nationwide and for six large cities. We also have the breakdowns among these for residential, commercial, and industrial land. This breakdown allows us to see which types of land were particularly important for the boom-bust cycle that we describe.

Table 4.1 *The Trigger*

Topic	Evidence
Real estate market crash	Urban land price index

During the initial phases of the liquidity shock, we expect the decline in demand for assets with low liquidity to lead to lower prices for such assets (see Table 4.2). (To recall why, refer to Figure 3.3.) For the case of Japan, we examine prices in residential and overall urban land, since both types of land are relatively less liquid assets. To sell, say, a given plot in Tokyo, a seller must be matched with a buyer interested in that particular plot. The two parties must then agree on a price and complete the transaction. For someone interested in an asset that can be converted into cash quickly, land is clearly not an asset that would be of much use.

Table 4.2   *Change in Liquidity Demanded Throughout the Economy*

Topic	Evidence
Decrease in Demand for Assets with Low Liquidity → Fall in Price of Low Liquidity Assets	
Residential Real Estate	Urban residential land price index
Land Prices	Urban land price index
Increase in Demand for High Liquidity Assets → Increase in Price of High Liquidity Assets	
Short-term federal government debt	Yields on short-term Japanese Government Bonds (JGBs)
Increase in Demand for High Versus Low Liquidity Assets → Increase in Price of High Liquidity Assets Relative to Price of Low Liquidity Assets	
Long-term versus short-term government debt	Yields on one-year versus 20-year Japanese Government Bonds (JGBs)
Government bonds relative to corporate bonds	Risk premium on lending (spread between prime rate and short-term government securities)

Conversely, prices of assets with very high liquidity would be expected to rise, so we also consider the prices of assets with very high liquidity. For the case of Japan, Japanese Government Bonds (JGBs) represent borrowing by Japan's central government. These bonds are highly liquid—they can easily be converted into cash at a predictable price.

Finally, we explore changes in the prices of assets with very high liquidity relative to the prices of assets with somewhat lower liquidity. The first comparison that we make is between yields on 20-year and yields on one-year JGBs. Here, the one-year JGB is considered the more liquid of the two. Because it will be paid off soon, others are happy to purchase it at a predictable price. Thus, when we see a bigger fall in the yield on the one-year than in the yield on the 20-year, it means that the yield on the less liquid (20-year) has increased relative to the yield on the more liquid (one-year). Recalling that yields move in the opposite direction of prices, this in turn means that the price of the less liquid 20-year has fallen relative to the price on the more liquid one-year—liquidity has become more valuable.[5]

We also examine data on *spreads,* the difference between the rates on two different securities. A larger spread implies that the two different securities are viewed as being very different, with one more desirable than the other. A small spread means that the two securities are priced closely to each other. We examine the spread between the rate on short-term corporate borrowing and the rate on short-term government securities. Here, an increase in the spread is what we would expect when liquidity becomes more coveted, since it means that the rate on the less liquid corporate borrowing has increased relative to the rate on the very liquid short-term government security. Another way to think about it is as meaning that the prices of the less liquid corporate bonds are falling relative to the price on the very liquid short-term government securities.

Next, we examine changes in bank balance sheets (see Table 4.3) to see whether the changes that we would expect to occur in a liquidity crisis happened in the case of Japan's Lost Decade. We would expect to see a fall in the value of bank assets with low liquidity, namely loans; bank deposits either falling or changing little; and a decline in bank equity. For the case of Japan, we look directly at the some of these main categories of bank balance sheets—assets with low liquidity (loans), banks' main liability (deposits), and the value of a bank's equity (stockholders' equity).

Table 4.3   *Changes in Bank Balance Sheets*

Topic	Evidence
Fall in Value of Bank Assets with Low Liquidity	
Bank loans	Bank loans by all domestically licensed banks in Japan
Bank Deposits Falling or No Change	
Bank deposits	Total deposits for all domestically licensed banks in Japan
Decline in Bank Equity	
Bank equity	Stockholders' equity for all domestically licensed banks in Japan
Overall Bank Viability	
Nonperforming loans	Size of nonperforming loans

We also look at overall indicators of the status of the banking sector. For one, we are interested in the extent of loans that have a higher probability of not being repaid, so-called nonperforming loans (NPLs). The definition used by Japanese banks and authorities shifted over time, but generally it included loans that were extended to enterprises that have now failed and loans with payments that were past due. It is important to examine this information for two reasons. First, it tells us about the overall health of the banking sector; if there is a high ratio of nonperforming loans to total loans, it means that banks are likely to suffer losses in the future. This status could impact banks' current behavior by making them hesitant to extend new loans, since there is a high probability that the current loans will never be repaid. This information is also of interest because it conveys the extent of the evergreening problem discussed earlier. We also provide some discussion of some of the efforts made by the Japanese government to handle the problems in the banking sector.

Faced with changes in its balance sheet discussed above, a bank must take action to shore up its position (see Table 4.4). It could for instance shift away from low liquidity assets, and we look to data on bank holdings of low liquidity assets to see whether they decline. For the case of Japan, we examine data on the value of total loans by all domestically licensed banks in Japan. We also consider bank holdings of assets with very high liquidity. Here, we focus on the most liquid of assets—cash—in addition to government securities, which are also very liquid since they are easy to sell at a predictable price at any point in time. Finally, we have information on the ratio of banks' highly liquid reserves—cash and deposits with the Central Bank—to their assets that are claims on (i.e., loans to) the private sector and others. If this ratio is high, it suggests that banks are keeping their assets as liquid as possible, rather than lending them out in ways that might reduce their liquidity.

Table 4.4 *Banks Change Activities to Bolster Balance Sheet*

Topic	Evidence
Reduce lending and/or Sell Assets with Low Liquidity	
Holdings of assets with low liquidity	Value of total loans by domestically licensed banks
Increase in Holdings of Assets with High Liquidity	
Holdings of assets with very high liquidity	Value of cash holdings of domestically licensed banks
	Value of central government securities holdings of domestically licensed banks
Increase Holdings of High Liquidity Relative to Low Liquidity Assets	
Fraction of high liquidity relative to low liquidity assets	Bank liquid reserves to bank assets ratio (percent)

As noted in Table 4.5, the changes in bank behavior induced by the liquidity shock in turn impact the availability of funds throughout the economy. For the case of Japan, the timing of this impact is complicated by the evergreening discussed in the previous section.

Although banks were hurt by the events of 1989 and the general downturn in the economy, they often chose to "sweep under the rug" many of the issues that they faced. Rather than quickly turning to high liquidity assets, as happened with the U.S. Great Depression, Japanese banks instead continued to roll over troubled loans, creating a cadre of what have been called *"zombie firms."*[6] These firms existed, but were no longer thriving corporate entities. This meant that the banks, and essentially the entire economy, were putting off painful adjustment and, at the same time, were keeping any available funds locked up with unproductive, unsustainable borrowers. This behavior likely lengthened the time during which Japan grew only anemically— its Lost Decade.

Table 4.5 *Effect on Liquidity and Availability of Funds Throughout the Economy*

Topic	Evidence
General Decline in Availability of Funds for Assets with Low Liquidity	
Lending to households	Outstanding loans to households
Availability of funds to corporate sector	Firm perception of lender attitude
Loans outstanding to corporate sector	Loans outstanding by industry
Availability of Credit to Overall Economy	
General availability of credit	Domestic credit to the private sector

In any case, we do eventually observe that fewer funds become available for assets with low liquidity. We examine outstanding loans to households; a decline in such lending would imply net tightening of credit to this group. We also discuss loans outstanding to different corporate sectors and the results of an important survey of the corporate sector conducted by the Bank of Japan. One of the questions on this survey asks whether firms view credit as being tight or readily available. With a *credit crunch*, we expect firms to view credit as being tight. Finally, as an indicator of overall credit availability we consider total domestic credit to the private sector. This should tell us generally how available credit is within the economy.

Finally, in the final phase of a liquidity crisis, we expect the impact of the shrinking of credit to be felt throughout the real economy (see Table 4.6). To illustrate this stage of the crisis, we again focus especially on real estate and construction—sectors that generally require credit to function but that need this credit for assets (building, homes, etc.) with relatively low liquidity. New housing starts tell us about whether new activity is being undertaken, which would require financing to get started. Even more illuminating, we also have information on new housing starts by source of funding—public versus private. Japan pumped massive amounts of fiscal stimulus into the economy during the 1990s, so to gauge the impact of the credit situation on private sector economic activity, it is important to distinguish between privately and publicly funded activity.

Table 4.6 *Real Effects of Decline in Liquidity Observed Throughout the Economy*

Topic	Evidence
Decline in Activity in Sectors Requiring Funding, but Considered to Have Relatively Low Liquidity	
Activity in construction	New housing starts overall
	New housing starts by source of funding
Activity in real estate	Real estate transactions
Overall Economic Activity	
Gross Domestic Product (GDP)	Real GDP
Overall Price Trends	
Inflation and deflation	Domestic Corporate Goods Price Index
	Consumer Price Index
Employment and Unemployment	
Unemployment rate	Unemployment rate

To learn about the state of the broader economy, we consider Gross Domestic Product (GDP) and unemployment, just as we did for the case of the Great Depression. (GDP is the broadest measure of all the economic activity taking place in a country, while the unemployment rate tells us about jobs.) Finally, we examine trends in prices throughout the decade. All these measures, taken together, provide a good idea of the overall level of economic activity in the country after the liquidity shock hit.

4.3 Setting the Stage for the Trigger— the Background to Japan's Lost Decade

In a way strikingly similar to the U.S. Great Depression, Japan's Lost Decade was preceded by a period of boom, a time termed the *bubble period* that took place between 1987 and 1990.

One factor feeding the explosion in asset markets during that time was most surely Japan's image as the rising star of the world economy.[7] As one example, a 1988 book titled *The Japanese Century* opened with, "We are on the threshold of the Japanese Century."[8] Another book of 1988, *Trading Places: How We Allowed Japan to Take the Lead*, noted "the United States is rapidly passing economic hegemony to Japan."[9] That same book provides a hint of the confidence in Japan not only abroad but within its own borders—the author quotes Takushin Yamamoto, then president of Fujitsu, as stating in September 1986 "U.S. companies have not been able to beat Japan up to now because they don't understand Japanese competition."[10] Other titles of that era that indicate Japan's image include *The Competition: Dealing with Japan* and *Beyond Capitalism: The Japanese Model of Market Economics.*[11]

A factor supporting the bubble was easy monetary policy by the Bank of Japan (BOJ). Beginning in 1986, the BOJ lowered the official discount rate from 5% in January 1986 to 2.5% in February 1987—a reduction of 250 basis points in little more than a year. These moves were done in large part as a component of economic policy coordination with a few other countries, including the United States. Broadly speaking, the aim was to prevent further appreciation of the U.S. dollar and to coordinate macroeconomic policy across countries. Another motivation for the rate adjustments was Japan's increasing concern about its trade surplus with the United States. The trade deficit had led to protectionist threats from the U.S. Congress and increasing trade friction between the two countries. Easy monetary policy was intended to stimulate domestic demand in Japan, thereby easing the pressure on bilateral trade with the United States. Japan was also concerned about excessive appreciation of the yen.[12]

A number of important changes in the financial sector also contributed to the bubble. Throughout the 1980s, Japan instituted a series of actions deregulating financial markets. For one, the government gradually lifted ceilings on interest rates for deposits. In addition, rules affecting the traditional borrowers of Japanese banks changed substantially.[13] Historically, Japanese banks had close relationships with their most important borrowers—large Japanese corporations. However, in the 1980s other funding avenues opened to these large firms. First, foreign exchange transactions became more freely available, allowing Japanese firms to more easily tap foreign bond markets. Second, a domestic commercial paper market was created in 1987, and the rules on collateral for issuing bonds, which had begun to ease in the late 1970s, became even less binding. Finally, issuing stock became much easier, opening another potential channel for corporate finance. Taken together, these changes meant that Japanese banks' traditional borrowers—large Japanese corporations—had an expanding array of possible avenues for raising funds.[14]

Faced with deregulated interest rates and loss of their traditional borrowers, Japanese banks turned to increasingly aggressive lending.[15] For example, researchers Kashyap and Hoshi emphasize the increasing importance of lending to small businesses and for real estate purchases. Figures 4.2 and 4.3 illustrate this trend.[16] Figure 4.2 shows that the share of bank lending going to small firms began to increase in the mid 1970s, with another jump up during the late 1980s. As for loans to real estate, Figure 4.3 shows that this share just about doubled during the course of the 1980s. Such lending provided fuel to the emerging asset price bubble.

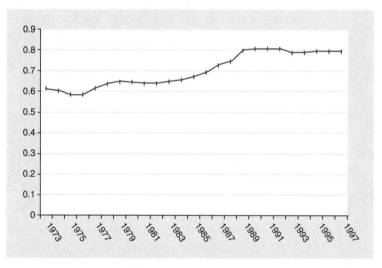

Source: Bank of Japan, *Economic Statistics Annual*, various issues.
Takeo Hoshi and Anil Kashyap (2000) "The Japanese Banking Crisis: Where Did It Come From and How Will It End?" in Bernanke, Ben S., and Julio J. Rotemberg, eds., *NBER Macroeconomics Annual 1999*, figure 3, page 162, © 2000 NBER and Massachusetts Institute of Technology, by permission of The MIT Press.[17]

Figure 4.2 *Lending to small firms*

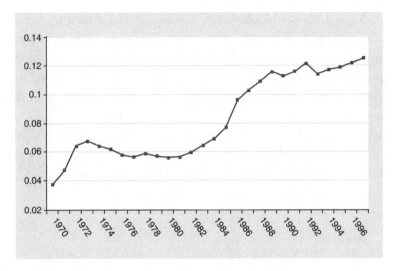

Source: Bank of Japan, *Economic Statistics Annual*, various issues.
Takeo Hoshi and Anil Kashyap (2000) "The Japanese Banking Crisis: Where Did
It Come From and How Will It End?" in Bernanke, Ben S., and Julio J. Rotemberg,
eds., *NBER Macroeconomics Annual 1999*, figure 4, page 163, © 2000 NBER and
Massachusetts Institute of Technology, by permission of The MIT Press.

Figure 4.3   *Lending to real estate*

For the purposes of our own analysis, an additional critical aspect
of such changes in bank behavior is what happens to the asset side of
bank balance sheets. From a liquidity perspective, an increase in loans
for real estate purchases and to small businesses implies an increase
in illiquidity risk, a key feature of the subsequent crisis faced by
Japanese banks and the economy as a whole. In addition, given the
huge increase in the prices of real estate in the late 1980s, banks'
assets came to be increasingly based on artificially high values in one
specific sector.[18] They also became increasingly vulnerable to any
downward movement in the price of real estate.

Thus, fueled by excessive optimism about Japan's future prospects, loose money, and changes in financial regulation, Japan's economy experienced two massive bubbles during the late 1980s, in stocks and in real estate.[19] Figure 4.4 shows growth in the Nikkei index of stocks on the Tokyo Stock Exchange. (This index incorporates the prices of 225 different stocks.) The Tokyo Stock Exchange exploded in the late 1980s, peaking in December 1989. As for real estate, Figure 4.5 shows the growth in land prices in the six largest cities in Japan. The price of commercial land in these six large urban areas grew an astonishing 450% between 1981 and 1990. Even more shocking, these prices grew by 28% in just one year—between 1989 and 1990.

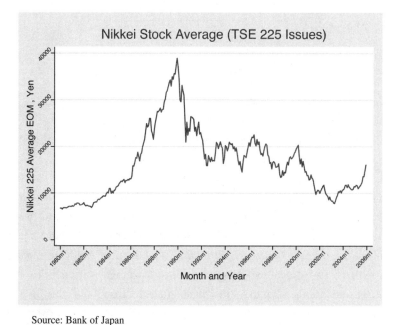

Source: Bank of Japan

Figure 4.4 *Nikkei*

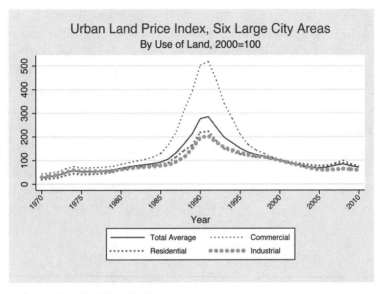

Source: Japan Real Estate Institute
6 large city areas refer to ku-area of Tokyo, Yokohama, Nagoya, Kyoto, Osaka, and Kobe.

Figure 4.5 *Urban land price index, six large city areas*

The Japanese government became increasingly concerned about what it recognized as unsustainable asset price growth. Thus, the Bank of Japan initiated a series of hikes in the official discount rate starting in May 1989.[20] Then, in 1990, the Ministry of Finance introduced limits on bank lending to the real estate sector.[21] Over the next year or so, the bubbles in both the stock market and in real estate burst, and Japan entered a decade of anemic growth. Indeed, after enjoying strong growth for two decades—around 4.5% on average during both the 1970s and 1980s—Japan's growth stagnated throughout the 1990s, with the economy expanding at only about 1.5% on average over the ten years, as shown in Figure 4.6.[22] This decade of low growth has been termed the Lost Decade, following as it did upon such robust growth and expectations of future potential for the Japanese economy. The next sections of this chapter trace out the evidence regarding the liquidity-related aspects of the Lost Decade. As in the previous chapter, our discussion follows the phases described previously. We first note the trigger (1), then changes in the liquidity demanded throughout the economy (2), changes in bank balance sheets (3), changes in bank activity (4), the effect on liquidity and availability of funds throughout the economy (5), and finally, the real effects of the decline in liquidity as observed throughout the economy (6).

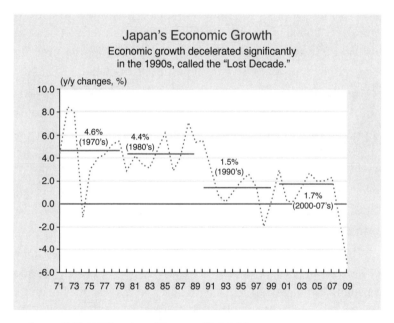

Source: Cabinet Office, *Annual Report on National Accounts*.
Masaaki Shirakawa, "Uniqueness or similarity? Japan's post-bubble experience in monetary policy studies," keynote address by Mr. Masaaki Shirakawa, Governor of the Bank of Japan, at the Second International Journal of Central Banking (IJCB) Fall Conference, Tokyo, 16 September 2010. http://www.bis.org/review/r100920b.pdf?frames=0.

Figure 4.6 *Economic growth*

4.4 Stage 1: The Trigger

The plummet in the real estate market, particularly in real estate in large cities, constituted the signal event that led to the liquidity crisis of Japan's Lost Decade. Referring back to Figure 4.5, in six large urban areas in Japan (Tokyo, Yokohama, Nagoya, Kyoto, Osaka, and Kobe) the overall price of urban land fell by 16% between 1991 and 1992. For the price of residential land in these six large urban areas, the drop was 18% between 1991 and 1992. To give a sense of the magnitude of this drop, a piece of housing land that was worth the yen equivalent of $500,000 in 1991 would be worth only $410,000 just one year later. Given that prices had risen steadily over the preceding decade, this drop would have been particularly notable.

Interestingly, urban land prices nationwide also dropped, but both the timing and the magnitude were different from the pattern for prices in the six large cities. Figure 4.7 shows that the overall index nationwide fell only about 2% between 1991 and 1992. We return to this difference between nationwide and large cities later, but, for now, the difference supports our conclusion that the trigger for this liquidity crisis was the plummet in the real estate market in large cities in Japan.

This decline in land prices had a particularly heavy impact because of the changes in bank activities that we discussed previously, namely the increased focus on lending to real estate. Related, an increasing portion of bank loans were loans with real estate as collateral. These changes made the banking sector particularly vulnerable to the plummet in the real estate market that served as the trigger to Japan's liquidity crisis.

4.5 Stage 2: Change in Liquidity Demanded Throughout the Economy

As with the case of the U.S. Great Depression, the crash in the real estate market led to a shift in liquidity demanded throughout the economy. Broadly speaking, there was an increase in demand for high-liquidity assets and a decline in demand for low liquidity assets. In this section, we describe how this increase was reflected in asset prices and financial markets during this era.

One sign that we look to as indicating a liquidity-crisis-related recession is a decline in the absolute price of assets with low liquidity, such as land. Figures 4.5 and 4.7 show the urban land price index, both for large cities and nationwide. We alluded to differences in timing between what happened to land prices in large cities as compared to land prices for the country as a whole. Indeed, between 1991 and 1992, the nationwide index was fairly flat, while the overall price of urban land in the six large city areas fell by 16%. Figure 4.8 provides another illustration of this point. It shows this same index for the six large city areas and then for all urban areas in the country outside those six large cities. The vertical lines indicate 1991 and 1992. We can see that the index for the six cities plunged between 1991 and 1992 (the "trigger"), while it was flat outside the six large cities.

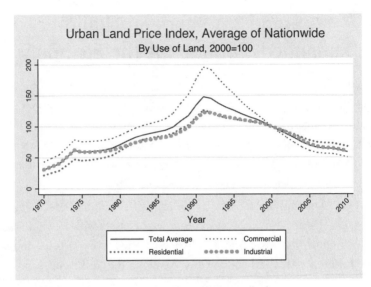

Source: Japan Ministry of Internal Affairs and Communication

Figure 4.7   *Urban land price index, nationwide*

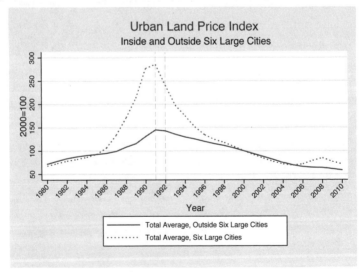

Source: Japan Real Estate Institute

6 large city areas refer to ku-area of Tokyo, Yokohama, Nagoya, Kyoto, Osaka and Kobe.
Figure 4.8   *Urban land price, inside and outside large cities*

In 1993, however, declines around the country accelerated. The large city index continued to fall. By 1995, the overall nationwide index had fallen 15% from its peak in 1991, while the large city index had fallen 47%. Particularly remarkable, the plummet in real estate in Japan continued throughout the 1990s and into the next century. By 2010, the overall index of urban land prices throughout the country had fallen by just more than 60%, putting the price level back to around where it had been in 1975, something that is clear from Figure 4.7.

Along with a decline in the price of assets with low liquidity, we expect to see an increase in the price of assets with high liquidity. As investors look for the most liquid places to park their funds, they drive up the prices in the markets for high-liquidity assets. To illustrate, Figure 4.9 shows the interest rates on one-, five-, ten-, and twenty-year Japanese Government Bonds (JGBs). The rates on all these declined over this time period, meaning there was an increase in their prices. With the one-year JGB being the most highly liquid of these assets, we would expect the most marked decline in its rate with the onset of a liquidity shock. Indeed, after peaking in September 1990, the one-year rate declined by about 270 basis points by just one year later. Less liquid, longer term bonds also exhibited a decline, but by less than was the case for the one-year instrument; the twenty-year JGB, for example, declined by only about 120 basis points.

When we consider the increase in the price of a very liquid asset relative to a less liquid asset, we also see the particularly high premium placed on the most liquid of assets. Figure 4.10 shows the spread between the prime rate to the private sector and the rate on short-term government securities. The prime rate to the private sector represents the rate charged to highly rated corporate borrowers, while the rate on short-term government securities is the rate charged to the government. The spread is the difference between the two rates.

A higher spread means that private-sector borrowers have to pay more, relative to the government rate. It is also equivalent to a decline in the price of the loan to the corporate sector relative to one to the government. Here, we see a jump in this spread in 1990. Since the government instrument is more liquid than the corporate one, this rise is consistent with an increase in the price of the more liquid asset relative to the less liquid asset.

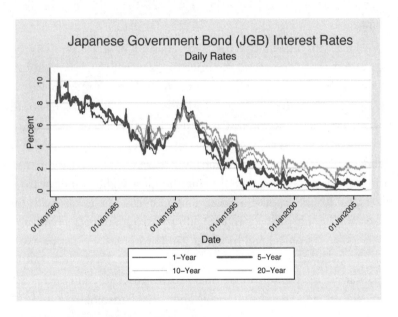

Source: Ministry of Finance of Japan

Figure 4.9   *Yields on JGBs*

The changes that we document here illustrate the effects of a change in liquidity demand throughout the economy. With a steep premium now placed on liquid assets, we observe a dramatic fall in the price of the asset with low liquidity (real estate), along with a rise in the price of the highly liquid asset (JGBs).

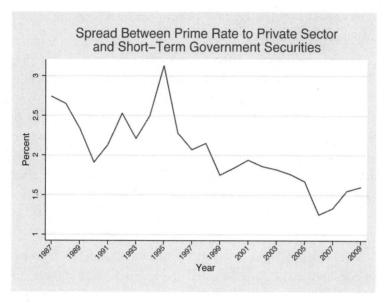

Source: World Bank

Figure 4.10 *Spread between prime rate and short-term government securities*

In the next section, we see how these changes in prices in asset markets impact bank balance sheets, the third phase in the flowchart shown previously in Figure 4.1.

4.6 Stage 3: Changes in Bank Balance Sheets

We examine bank balance sheets to see whether the changes that we would expect to occur in a liquidity crisis happened in the case of Japan's Lost Decade. We would expect to see a fall in the value of bank assets with low liquidity, namely loans; bank deposits either falling or changing little; and a decline in bank equity. For the case of Japan, we look directly at some of the main categories of bank balance sheets—assets with low liquidity (loans), liabilities, and the value of bank equity (capital stock).

For the case of Japan, interpretation of the data is complicated for at least two reasons. First, as is normally the case, the data that we have on the assets on bank balance sheets are generally "book value," so any decline in the inherent value of a loan due to the fall in the price of an asset may not show up immediately in the value of loans. Furthermore, financial authorities at one point during the crisis changed the rules on how banks could record the value of assets, allowing them to choose either market or book values. Banks chose the option that would present their books in the most favorable light possible, making interpretation of the data even more difficult.

Second, since Japanese banks commonly reloaned to borrowers that might otherwise have defaulted, the apparent value of their loans was further propped up. (This practice was described earlier in our discussion on evergreening.) If defaults were allowed to proceed, the value of loans would fall immediately. By keeping the borrower current on the loan, on the other hand, the bank maintained that asset on its balance sheet at book value. Given the complexities of the situation in Japan, we present the data and events in three stages: 1990 to 1993, 1993 to 1997, and late 1997 and later.

1990-1993

The initial stage took place between 1990 and 1993, when the initial impact of the plunge in asset prices hit the financial sector, although many problems still were hidden by evergreening. Figure 4.11 provides the value of loans on the books of domestically licensed banks in Japan between 1987 and 1993. This value increased substantially in the last three years of the 1980s, growing just over 30% between 1987 and 1990. Thereafter, the rate of growth slowed substantially, with the total value of loans growing only 8% between 1990 and 1993. Thus, rather than a decline in loans, we observe a significant slowing in the rate of growth in these loans in the initial years of the crisis.

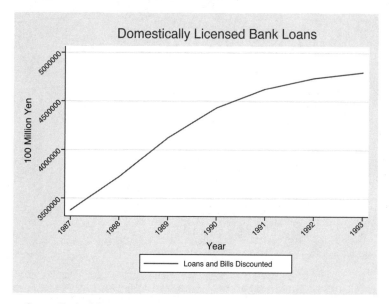

Source: Bank of Japan

Figure 4.11 *Bank loans*

As for the liabilities side of the balance sheet, the top panel of Figure 4.12 shows total deposits at domestically licensed banks. Here, the value of deposits fell after peaking in 1990, falling by about 8% between 1990 and 1993. As shown in the bottom panel, however, other components of the liabilities side rose; banks increased both borrowing (from the Bank of Japan and from other financial institutions) and debenture issuance. Borrowings increased by 82%, while debentures rose by 8% between 1987 and 1993. During this time period, bank capital rose just a bit.

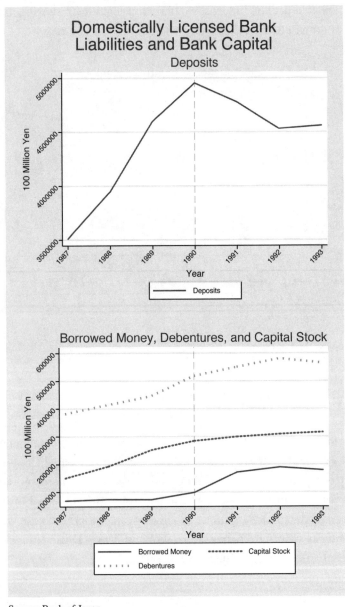

Source: Bank of Japan

Figure 4.12 *Bank liabilities and capital*

1993-1997

During the initial stage, banks had continued to extend loans to troubled borrowers, in part out of the hope that asset markets would soon rebound. As a result, most banks did not take the implied losses on their books early on, and the extent of the underlying weakness in the financial sector did not surface until around 1993, when we date the beginning of our second stage. At that point, certain financial institutions began to show signs of trouble—the *jusen*. *Jusen* were lending institutions created by Japanese banks and focused on lending for home mortgages and for real estate. Thus, they were especially hard hit by the bursting of the bubble in the real estate market. Between 1993 and 1996, the government made a number of unsuccessful attempts to rehabilitate and restructure the *jusen*, but in mid-1995, the losses of the *jusen* were estimated by the Ministry of Finance to have reached ¥6.4 trillion. They were eventually liquidated in 1996, and their assets and liabilities were taken over by the newly formed Housing Loan Administration Corporation.[23]

The failure of the *jusen* is important to understanding the liquidity crisis in Japan, for a number of reasons. First, as the initial institutions to show signs of trouble, their failure gave an indication of the much larger problems soon to follow. Second, *jusen* were institutions that had been founded by banks and other financial institutions in the 1970s. So, when the *jusen* went under, the founding banks, as well as banks that had lent to the *jusen*, took losses, thereby having a direct impact on bank balance sheets. Finally, some public funds (¥0.68 trillion) were used to facilitate liquidation of these institutions. This injection of public money outraged the populace, since the government had repeatedly promised that public funds would not be needed to resolve the *jusen* problem. This resentment may have increased the reluctance of the Japanese government to use public funds for subsequent bailouts.[24]

Late 1997 and Later

Kicking off the third stage in our description is the failure of Sanyo Securities in November 1997. Although Sanyo was not a bank per se, it was a borrower on the interbank call market. When it went under, it defaulted on its loans in the interbank market—the first ever default in the interbank market in Japan. This default jolted the interbank market. Banks became increasingly reluctant to lend to other banks. Additional shocks hit the system during November 1997 with a string of failures of financial institutions. During that month, after the failure of Sanyo Securities (November 3), Hokkaido Takushoku Bank (November 17), Yamaichi Securities (November 24), and Tokuyo City Bank (November 26) also failed. Depositors, panicked by this string of failures, moved to withdraw their savings.[25]

Figure 4.13 shows the *Japan premium* at that time. The Japan premium is the difference between the costs of borrowing on the interbank market for Japanese banks versus the costs of interbank borrowing for non-Japanese banks. An increase in the premium means that Japanese banks have to pay more relative to non-Japanese banks and indicates that markets believe that there is a higher risk of default by Japanese banks.[26] Figure 4.13 shows the spike in the Japan premium at the end of 1997, this time of turmoil in the interbank market in Japan.

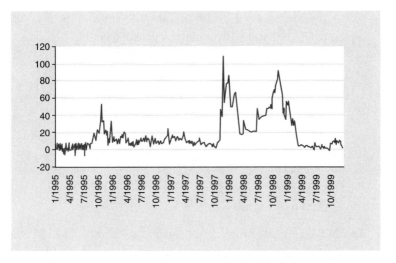

Source: Hoshi, Takeo, and Anil K Kashyap (2010) "Will the U.S. bank recapitalization succeed? Eight lessons from Japan." *Journal of Financial Economics* 97(3) 398-417.

The figure shows the Japan premium calculated as the difference between three-month Eurodollar Tokyo Interbank Borrowing Rate (TIBOR) and the three-month Eurodollar London Interbank Borrowing Rate (LIBOR). We thank Kimie Harada and Takatoshi Ito for providing data for the figure. Eurodollar TIBOR is calculated by QUICK (a Japanese data provider) as the average interbank rate of the middle 9 of the 13 reference banks. (The highest two and the lowest two banks are excluded.) The 13 banks include 2 non-Japanese banks, but their rates were almost always excluded as the two lowest, effectively making TIBOR the average rate for Japanese banks. Eurodollar LIBOR is calculated by the British Bankers Association as the average interbank rate of the middle 8 of the 16 reference banks. Three Japanese banks are included in the 16 reference banks, but their rates were almost always excluded as 3 of the 4 highest rates, effectively making LIBOR the average rate for non-Japanese banks. See Ito and Harada (2005). The units are basis points.

Figure 4.13 *The Japan premium*

Faced with the potential collapse of the Japanese financial system, the Japanese Minister of Finance and the Governor of the Bank of Japan jointly issued the following statement:

1. We, the Minister of Finance and the Governor of the Bank of Japan, would like to reaffirm our strong will to fulfill the commitment to ensure the stability of interbank transactions as well as to fully protect deposits....

2. The financial system is the basis of the economy and society. We will take all possible measures to ensure its stability.

3. Therefore, we are determined to provide liquidity in a sufficient and decisive manner in order to prevent any delay in payments of deposits and other liabilities of financial institutions. We strongly request people not to be misguided by groundless rumors and to act sensibly.[27]

Another factor affecting bank behavior at the end of 1997 was recent and pending heightened stringency in bank inspections by Japanese authorities. A new Prompt Corrective Action framework was slated to be implemented in April 1998. In the months preceding this, banking authorities stepped up their inspections, including verifying that financial institutions were improving their internal assessment methods.[28] Furthermore, the new Financial Supervisory Agency was to begin operations in June 1998. Illustrating the new attitude toward banking institutions, the head of the Bank of Japan (Japan's Central Bank) Yasuo Matsushita, in a speech on December 12, 1997, noted, "Depositors, creditors, and other market participants are scrutinizing the financial conditions of Japanese financial institutions with increasing severity, and the scheduled introduction of Prompt Corrective Action in April 1998...are likely to encourage such tendency. Therefore, it is vital that individual financial institutions accelerate the disposal of nonperforming loans and the implementation of restructuring measures to ensure the market's confidence."[29] This increased scrutiny of bank balance sheets may have also induced banks to turn away from lending as they worked to clean up their financial positions to satisfy a heightened level of diligence on the part of regulatory authorities.

Taken together, these three factors—the first-ever default on the interbank market, the failures of multiple financial institutions, and recent and pending heightened scrutiny of banking institutions— served to shake the system out of the stasis that had been present since the initial bursting of the asset price bubble. Not until the confluence of these dramatic events do we observe the changes in bank activities that we would expect to accompany a liquidity crisis—nearly a decade after the initial shock to asset prices.

Faced with this turmoil in financial markets at the end of 1997, the government decided that a program of recapitalization was needed to prop up the Japanese financial system. The first injection occurred in March 1998, when ¥1.816 trillion was injected.[30] When that initial infusion failed to resolve the situation, further recapitalization programs followed, beginning in March 1999. This next chunk of public funds was accompanied by the requirement that banks provide a plan for returning to profitability.[31] Nevertheless, the system as a whole remained shaky. Banks continued to fail, with the government nationalizing some financial institutions. The government also continued its programs of buying up troubled assets, including, after 1999, from still-solvent financial institutions.[32]

Changes in the asset sides of bank balance sheets during this time period are particularly interesting. With the freezing in the interbank market at the end of 1997, the percent of assets placed in loans (see the bottom panel of Figure 4.14) declined dramatically, while the share in central government securities rose (see the top panel of Figure 4.14). This type of change is consistent with what we would expect to see as banks turn away from assets with low liquidity and toward assets with high liquidity, a point that we discuss in more detail in the following section.[33]

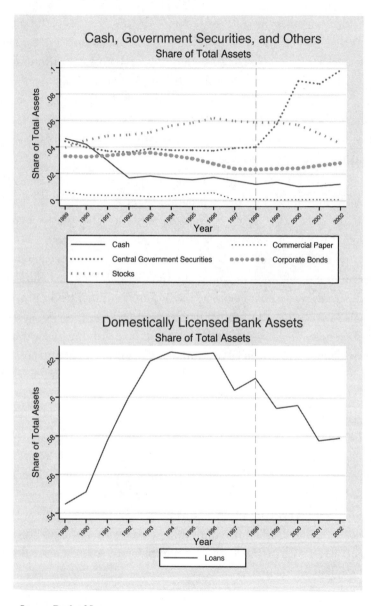

Source: Bank of Japan

Figure 4.14   *Bank assets by type of asset*

More information on the status of the banking sector in Japan during the 1990s is provided by the extent of the nonperforming loan (NPL) problem. The definition used by Japanese banks and authorities for NPLs shifted over time, but generally it included loans that were extended to enterprises that have failed and loans with payments that are past due. As previously discussed, the extent of NPLs tells us about the overall health of the banking sector. This status could impact their current behavior by making them hesitant to extend new loans, since there is a high probability that current loans will never be repaid. In addition, it conveys the extent of the evergreening problem discussed earlier.

Estimating the extent of the problem is difficult. Banks did not report information on NPLs before 1993, and thereafter definitions changed periodically. Figure 4.15 provides estimates from one analyst. The increases in 1995 and 1997 are at least partially attributable to changes in the definition of nonperforming loans, which was expanded in those years. These increases that came with the redefinitions undermined credibility in the veracity of the numbers that were being reported, heightening concerns about the health of the banking sector.

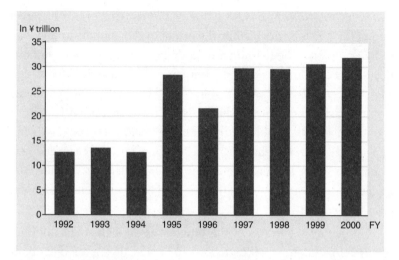

Source: Hiroshi Nakaso, "The financial crisis in Japan during the 1990s: how the Bank of Japan responded and the lessons learnt." Bank for International Settlement (BIS) Papers No 6, October 2001.
Note: Before FY 1994, the disclosed amount of NPLs was the total of "loans to legally bankrupt companies" and "loans past due for six months or more." From FY 1995 to FY 1996, the figures include the amount of "loans for which interest rates were reduced," which banks were required to disclose under the new rule, in addition to the previous categories. From FY 1997 to the present, the figures include "loans past due for three months or more" and "restructured loans." The category for "loans for which interest rates were reduced" was reclassified as a part of the "restructured loans."

Figure 4.15 *Nonperforming loans*

The International Monetary Fund (IMF) has also provided some information on the scope of the nonperforming loan problem. It has reported the ratio of NPLs to total loans to be 6.6% in 1995, 8.5% in 1998, and 7.9% in 2000.[34] Additional and more recent information is provided by Japan's Financial Services Agency. As shown in Figure 4.16, the ratio of NPLs to total loans remained elevated into the 2000s, peaking in March 2002 at 8.7%.[35,36] To give some basis for comparison, the ratio of nonperforming loans to total loans during the U.S. savings and loan crisis of 1980-1992 was about 4%.[37]

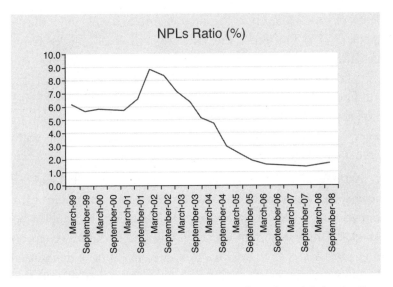

Source: Financial Services Agency of Japan, http://www.fsa.go.jp/en/regulated/npl/20090807.html.

Figure 4.16   *Nonperforming loans ratio*

4.7 Stage 4: Banks Change Activities to Bolster Balance Sheets

Faced with changes in balance sheets such as those discussed previously, banks must act to shore up their positions. However, as in the previous section, the complex set of regulatory and policy changes occurring in Japan throughout the 1990s complicate our analysis of bank activities during these years, particularly with regard to the timing of these changes.

For example, in late 1997, the government relaxed accounting standards for banks, allowing them to use either book or market value for their real estate and securities holdings. This change meant that, cosmetically, banks' balance sheets appeared to be in better shape. As one example, in March 1998, Dai-ichi Kangyo Bank went from a

141

capital ratio of 7.51% under the old standards to 9.09% under the new standards. For Fuji Bank, the shift was from 7.29% under the old standards to 9.41% under the new standards.[38] The change from below to above 8% is particularly important, since Japanese banks with foreign branches had been required to meet the Basel 8% minimum since early 1993.[39] This relaxation of standards also meant that banks' balance sheets were effectively "shored up" on the face of it, without any changes in behavior occurring at all.

Another important element, discussed in more detail earlier in the chapter, was evergreening. To delay the realization of losses from nonperforming loans, banks kept reloaning money to troubled borrowers.[40] Other important events during this era included government provision of both a virtual guarantee on all bank deposits and also of several rounds of funds for bank recapitalization. All told, these regulatory and policy elements meant that banks put off much of the balance sheet changes that we would expect to observe in the wake of a liquidity shock. In fact, not until 2002, when Heizo Takenaka took charge of Japan's Financial Services Agency, did Japan fully acknowledge and begin to deal with the problems in its financial sector.[41]

Nevertheless, the items on the balance sheets of Japanese banks did eventually illustrate the changes that we would expect to see. For example, one way in which banks could act to shore up their positions would be to shift away from low liquidity assets, such as loans. The top panel of Figure 4.17 provides data on the value of total loans by all domestically licensed banks in Japan, as a share of total assets. The drop-off in loan activity after 1998 that we discussed earlier is clear. Data from the longer time period also reveal that Japanese banks continued to shrink the share of loans in their asset portfolios through the end of the 1990s and well into the early 2000s. This share declined from 62% in 1995 to 54% in 2004—a fall of 13%. Further illustrating this point, Figure 4.18 shows changes in the value of bank loans from the previous year. Growth in bank loans slowed through the end of the

1990s, then began to shrink in 1998. Total bank loans continued to contract through the mid 2000s.

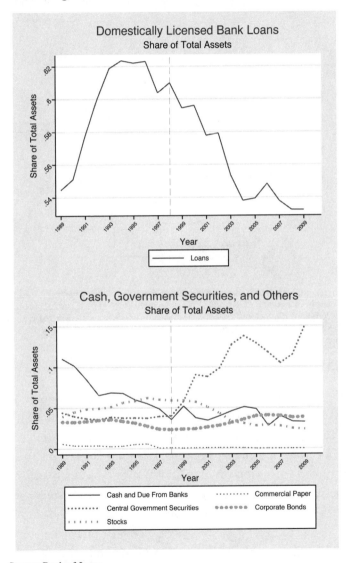

Source: Bank of Japan

Figure 4.17 *Domestically licensed banks assets, longer time period*

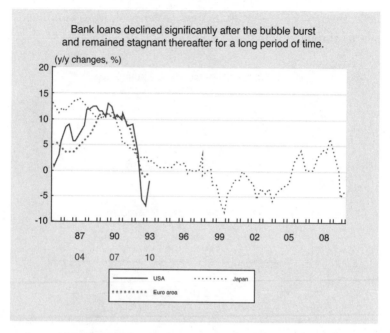

Source: Masaaki Shirakawa, "Uniqueness or similarity? Japan's post-bubble experience in monetary policy studies," Keynote address by Mr. Masaaki Shirakawa, Governor of the Bank of Japan, at the Second International Journal of Central Banking (IJCB) Fall Conference, Tokyo, 16 September 2010. http://www.bis.org/review/r100920b.pdf?frames=0.

Figure 4.18   *Bank loans*

We would also expect to see an increase in bank holdings of very liquid assets. The bottom panel of Figure 4.17 provides this information. The rise in the share of assets Japanese banks placed in government securities is striking. Between 1998 and 2004, the share grew from 4% to 14%—a growth rate of 243% over those six years. Indeed, it looks like two of the large capital injections by the Japanese government, in early 1998 and again in 1999, were stashed mostly in government securities, based on the large increases in bank holdings of Central Government Securities in those two years.

Comparing the top and bottom panels of Figure 4.17 provides some hint of the effects of the Japanese government's attempts to deal with bad loans as they worked to strengthen the financial system. In the late 1990s, the government began to buy nonperforming loans from banks more aggressively than it had before, a move that took these loans off the books of the selling banks. During that same time period, the share of bank assets going to central government securities increased tremendously, tripling between 1995 and 2005. This pattern suggests that, although the effects of the liquidity shock were long-delayed, they eventually emerged once banks were forced to cease relending to "zombie" firms. At that point, banks increased investments in central government securities, rather than expanding their loan portfolios, thereby illustrating the shift into assets with high liquidity that we would expect to observe in the wake of a liquidity shock.

As a final indicator, Figure 4.19 shows the ratio of banks' highly liquid reserves—cash and deposits with the Central Bank—to their assets that are claims on (i.e., loans to) the private sector and others. If this ratio is high, it suggests that banks are keeping their assets as liquid as possible, rather than lending them out in ways that might reduce their liquidity. This ratio for the case of Japan was under 1.00 throughout most of the 1990s. At the end of the decade, when underlying problems in the financial sector began to emerge and be dealt with, it began to climb dramatically, indicating an increasing preference for liquidity.

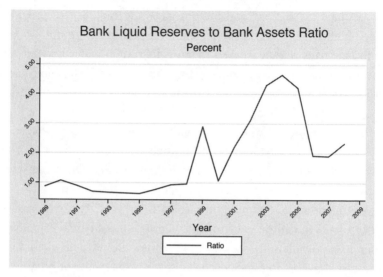

Source: The World Bank
Ratio of bank liquid reserves to bank assets is the ratio of domestic currency holdings and deposits with the monetary authorities to claims on other governments, nonfinancial public enterprises, the private sector, and other banking institutions.

Figure 4.19 *Liquid reserves to assets ratio*

On the liabilities side of the bank balance sheet, deposits grew between 1993 and 1995 (see top panel of Figure 4.20). However, a stream of shocks hit the system in late 1994 and in 1995; these shocks to deposits had important effects on the balance sheets of banks and the Japanese financial system as a whole.

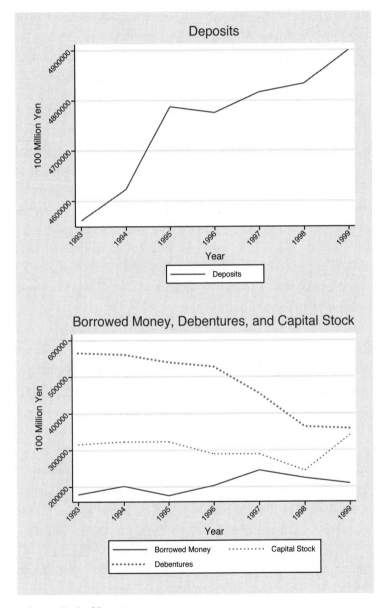

Source: Bank of Japan

Figure 4.20 *Bank liabilities and capital*

In December 1994, two urban financial institutions that had been taking deposits failed. Although depositors were made whole via a government package and creation of a new bank (Tokyo Kyoudou Bank), prior to these two failures at the end of 1994, deposit-taking institutions had not been allowed to go under. Subsequently, three more financial institutions went under in the summer of 1995. The *jusen* problem discussed earlier also came to a head around this time when the Ministry of Finance announced in the summer of 1995 that the losses of the *jusen* amounted to ¥6.4 trillion, far more than could be covered by the founding banks, and that 74% of the *jusen* loans were nonperforming.[42] Depositors reacted by shifting their savings away from banks with low credit ratings and into the government's Postal Savings System. As one indicator, between 1995 and 1996, growth in deposits at city banks (one group within the domestically licensed banks shown in Figure 4.20) was 0.06%, while growth in deposits in the Postal Savings System was 5.36%.[43]

Bank capital was also shaky during this period. As shown in the bottom panel of Figure 4.20, the value fell gradually until 1998, when the first of the government's capital injection programs occurred.

Thus, in the end, we did observe the changes that would be expected in the wake of a liquidity shock. Banks shifted away from low liquidity assets into assets with high liquidity. Bank deposits were fairly steady, but only with government reassurance and support. Similarly, bank capital was boosted by government intervention.

In hindsight, the prolonged crisis in Japan raises the question of why it took so long for the banking sector to return to health. Many analysts have addressed this question.[44] In short, the answer may be "too little, too late." Authorities attempted to resolve the situation via capital injections, purchases of troubled assets, and more stringent inspection requirements. However, many of these initiatives were far smaller than the extent of the problem and/or insufficiently critical of the health of banks. As a result, banks retained troubled assets on their books and confidence in the financial system remained low. A further pernicious element was the vicious macroeconomic cycle kicked off by the initial liquidity shock. With the changes in asset prices described previously and the tightening of credit, which we describe in the following section, the broader real economy was kicked into what became a spiraling decline in overall macroeconomic activity, which was in turn exacerbated by the tightening of bank credit. We discuss this issue further later in this chapter.

4.8 Stage 5: Effect on Liquidity and Availability of Credit Throughout the Economy

The delay in the impact of the liquidity shock in Japan is also apparent in information on the availability of credit throughout the economy. As discussed previously, the onset of the credit crunch in Japan was delayed by the tendency to roll over bad loans. Nevertheless, the data clearly illustrate this stage of a recession induced by a liquidity shock.

Speaking broadly, credit growth by domestic banks expanded slightly through 1996, when it increased about 1% from the previous year. Beginning in 1997, however, as the problems within the financial system became evident and banks began to fail, credit contracted. Credit extended by domestic banks fell by 0.08% in 1997 and by 0.90% in 1998.[45] Figure 4.21 provides a broad measure: all domestic credit provided to the private sector, as a percent of GDP.[46] The trends shown in this figure are consistent with the overall picture described throughout the chapter. There was a steep increase during the 1980s, followed by a level treading water during most of the 1990s. In the late 1990s, domestic credit increased sharply at the same time as the capital injection by the Japanese government. (Of note, a good portion of that capital injection reportedly went to low-performing firms as debt forgiveness.)[47] Once the banks began to finally deal with their problems, the amount of domestic credit extended to the private sector plummeted. We see credit shrinking, beginning in the late 1990s.

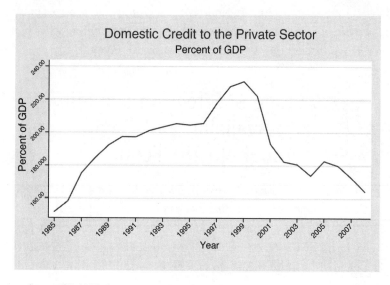

Source: World Bank
Domestic credit to private sector refers to financial resources provided to the private sector, such as through loans, purchases of nonequity securities, and trade credits and other accounts receivable, that establish a claim for repayment.

Figure 4.21 *Domestic credit to the private sector*

Turning to specific groups in the economy, Figure 4.22 shows lending to households. The value of outstanding consumer loans began to turn down in 1992, and continued declining throughout the decade. Figure 4.23 provides information on loans outstanding by industry. This figure is constructed such that the value of all loan categories is set to be 100 in the third quarter of 1994. Changes from 100 show increases and decreases in comparison to that base. This chart shows that loans to manufacturing were declining from 1994. Loans to real estate, on the other hand, actually increased through 1998, when they also began to fall. Construction loans were flat into 1999, when they also fell off. All told, Figure 4.23 suggests overall declining bank credit after 1998.

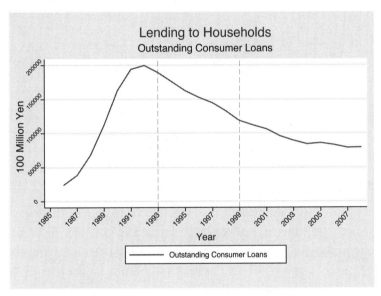

Source: Bank of Japan
Lines denote slight breaks in series.

Figure 4.22 *Lending to households by domestically licensed banks*

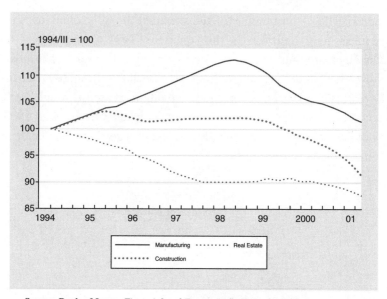

Source: Bank of Japan, *Financial and Economic Statistics Monthly*
Kunio Okina and Shigenori Shiratsuka, "Asset Price Bubbles, Price Stability, and
Monetary Policy: Japan's Experience," *Monetary and Economic Studies*, October 2002.

Figure 4.23   *Loans outstanding by industry*

Given the delay in changes in lending created by the tendency to
roll over bad loans, it is of particular interest to examine any perceptions on the part of firms of whether or not loans seem to be available.
Figure 4.24 shows a diffusion index for a question on firm perception
of the lending attitude of financial institutions. It takes the number
responding "accommodative" and subtracts the number responding
"severe." Thus, a negative number reflects an attitude by financial
institutions that is more severe than accommodative. This index is
shown for small firms, a group traditionally more dependent on bank
financing and to whom lending may be seen as generating a particularly illiquid asset for a bank. Small firms viewed financial institutions
as relatively loose during the early 1990s, the years in which evergreening was widespread. Once problems in the financial sector
became known and bad loans recognized toward the end of 1997,

small firms suddenly viewed lending conditions as being severe. This perception of severity continued into the middle of the next decade.

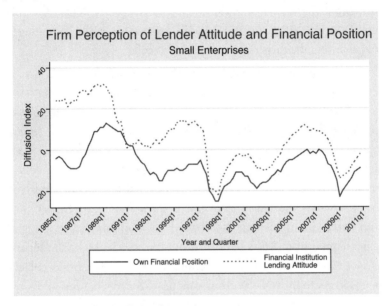

Source: Bank of Japan, Tankan Survey

Figure 4.24 *Lending attitude and financial position for small firms*

The other line in Figure 4.24 is a diffusion index indicating a firm's own estimation of its financial position. It takes the number responding "easy" and subtracts the number responding "tight." Thus, a negative number means that these small firms view their own financial positions as relatively tight. Small firms viewed their conditions as tight from 1991 onward. However, between 1990 and 1998, the time period during which banks were turning over bad loans, there is a distinct decoupling between firms' perception of lender attitude and their perceptions of their own financial position. While lending attitude was becoming more accommodative, firms' own financial positions were becoming tighter. This apparent contradiction could be explained by loans to troubled firms being rolled over to avoid default on these assets on banks' books. In any case, it is certainly clear that small firms viewed financial institutions as being severe on lending throughout the end of the 1990s and into the early 2000s, the time period during which Japanese banks were apparently beginning to deal with the aftermath of the liquidity shock.[48]

As a side note, in explaining the shrinkage of credit in the Japanese economy, we focus on the *supply side*, that is, whether banks are willing to loan funds to borrowers. Another perspective focuses on the *demand side*. In a 2003 book *Balance Sheet Recession: Japan's Struggle with Uncharted Economics and its Global Implications*, Richard Koo emphasizes the role of corporate balance sheets in explaining Japan's Lost Decade. He argues that Japan's corporate sector, hard hit by the fall in asset prices starting in 1990, turned away from profit maximization and toward "debt minimization." Figure 4.25, adapted from Koo's book, sets out the stages of what he terms a *balance sheet recession*. In his framework, an asset price collapse impels firms to move away from a mode of borrowing, investing, and expanding (*profit maximization*) and toward a mode of paying down debt to correct the balance sheet problems generated by the decline in asset prices (*debt minimization*). This change in corporate activity leads to a decline in aggregate demand, a weaker economy, and declining prices. The overall slowdown in economic activity further exacerbates balance sheet problems at firms and leads to further declines in asset prices. The struggles in the corporate sector hit the banking sector as loans held by banks become nonperforming.[49] Banks and their problems also play a key role in Koo's approach. His emphasis differs in that he argues that reduced demand for loans by the corporate sector, rather than an intentional shift by banks, underlies the decline in credit availability in the economy. Given that banks, but not other types of firms, are required by regulation to maintain a certain capital to assets ratio, we choose to focus on the supply side of the credit crunch and the behavior of banks.

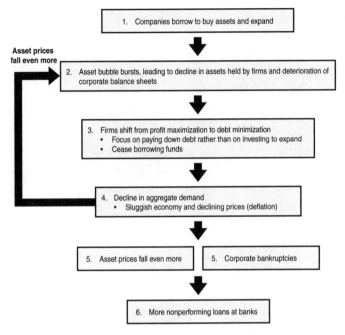

Figure 4.25 *Koo's balance sheet recession*

4.9 Stage 6: Real Effects of Decline in Liquidity Observed Throughout the Economy

As the final stage of a liquidity shock, we expect the impact of the shrinking of credit to be felt throughout the real economy. As the phrase goes, the shock moves "from Wall Street to Main Street." To illustrate this stage of the crisis, we focus especially on real estate and construction—sectors that generally require credit to function but that need this credit for assets (building, homes, etc.) with relatively low liquidity.

New housing starts tell us about whether new activity is being undertaken. Figure 4.26 shows total new housing starts in Japan. Overall, starts actually increased during the early 1990s, despite the large drop in land prices during these years, as discussed earlier and shown in Figure 4.7. Thereafter, starts declined dramatically, falling by 30% between 1996 and 2002.

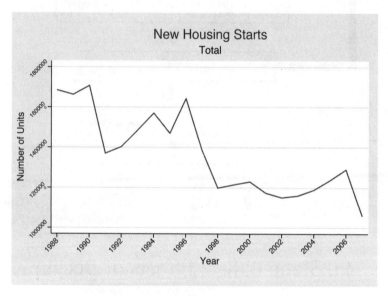

Source: Ministry of Land, Infrastructure, Transport and Tourism
http://www.mlit.go.jp/toukeijouhou/chojou/stat?e.htm.

Figure 4.26 *Total new housing starts*

To understand these trends, however, we need to look at new housing starts by source of funding—public versus private. Japan pumped massive amounts of fiscal stimulus into the economy during the 1990s, so to gauge the impact of the credit situation on private sector economic activity, it is important to distinguish between privately and publicly funded activity. As shown in Figure 4.27, the increase in the early '90s was entirely funded by the public sector. Housing starts funded privately in fact declined beginning in 1990 and, while volatile, generally declined throughout the decade. They picked up a bit at the beginning of the 2000s, but never exceeded the level reached in 1990.

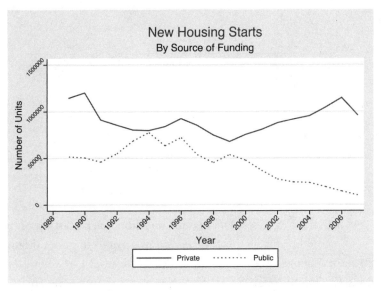

Source: Ministry of Land, Infrastructure, Transport and Tourism,
http://www.mlit.go.jp/toukeijouhou/chojou/stat?e.htm.

Figure 4.27 *New housing starts by source of funding*

As another indication of trends in real estate activity, Figure 4.28 shows the number of real estate transactions, or transfers of ownership throughout Japan. This indicator of activity plummeted after 1989 and remained subdued in the country as a whole into 2005.

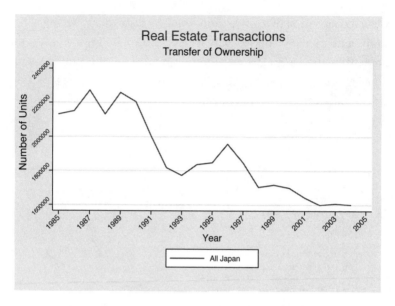

Source: Judicial System and Research Department, Minister's Secretariat, Ministry of Justice, Japan Stat Yearbook.

Figure 4.28   *Real estate transactions*

As with the U.S. Great Depression, an additional key aspect of the broader economy during this time period was trends in prices. Figure 4.29 shows changes in the Consumer Price Index (CPI) (General and Goods Excluding Fresh Food) from the previous year. Any changes below the zero line mean that prices are falling (deflation), while those above the zero line mean that prices are rising (inflation). The CPI for goods other than fresh food (which may be volatile and impacted by changes in weather and other factors) was generally falling throughout the last part of the 1990s and into the 2000s. Falling prices are a concern for a number of reasons. For one, deflation makes it harder for a borrower to pay back loans. In addition, if consumers put off purchases in anticipation of lower prices in the future, overall economic activity may be kicked into a downward spiral, as shrinking sales lead to further declines in prices and so on.

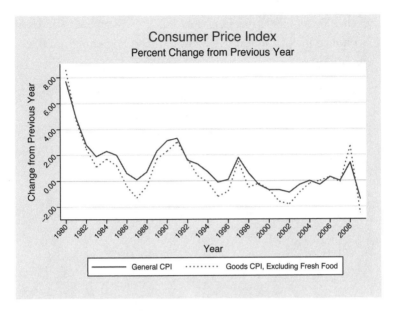

Source: Bank of Japan

Figure 4.29 *Deflation*

As discussed earlier and shown in Figure 4.7, there was also severe deflation in land prices throughout the Lost Decade and beyond. Falling land prices would undermine the value of any loans extended for real estate purchases. In addition, more generally, this general decline in prices would have the effect of reducing the value of the assets on bank balance sheets, as well as owners' perceptions of their own financial status.

Finally, two important measures of the state of the broader economy are Gross Domestic Product (GDP) and unemployment. As we discussed earlier and as shown in Figure 4.6, after enjoying strong growth for two decades—around 4.5% on average during both the 1970s and 1980s—Japan's growth stagnated throughout the 1990s, with the economy expanding at only about 1.5% on average over the ten years. Anemic growth continued into the 2000s, with the average between 2000 and 2007 reaching only 1.7%.[50] Consistent with declining economic growth, unemployment climbed beginning in 1992, as shown in Figure 4.30.

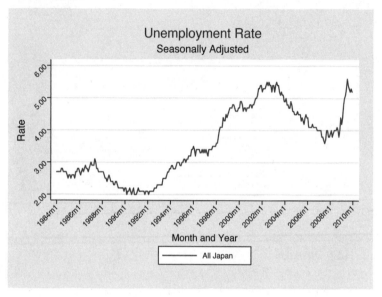

Source: Statistics Bureau and the Director-General for Policy Planning of Japan,
http://www.stat.go.jp/english/data/roudou/lngindex.htm.

Figure 4.30   *Unemployment*

All these measures—declining activity in real estate and construction, declining prices, slow growth, and employment—taken together provide a good idea of the overall level of economic activity in the country after the liquidity shock hit. Initially, there was stagnation as banks reloaned available funds to low quality borrowers. Growth continued to creep along as the effects of the initial liquidity shock were finally realized and banks put their funds into high liquidity assets. Robust expansion, however, ceased, and Japan to this day continues to experience anemic growth.

4.10 Conclusion: Japan's Lost Decade, a Liquidity Shock That Dragged On

As with Chapter 3 on the Great Depression in the United States, the evidence presented in this chapter has illustrated how a liquidity shock may be transmitted through the economy, as the banking sector shifts away from its traditional function of channeling funds from depositors to borrowers. The credit tightening in turn impacts the real sector and overall economic activity.

The case of Japan, however, also provides a few distinct contrasts. First, the extent and nature of the problems in Japan's financial sector were hidden for many years and allowed to fester. Assets remained trapped in low performing areas. Not only were problem loans not dealt with, but also any remaining value was not freed up to be redirected to more productive uses. This set the economy up for years and years of stagnation and left the country with a crisis in the financial system that was likely much larger and more severe than if it had dealt with the problems much earlier on.

Second, whereas we could point to a turn-around after the U.S. Great Depression, Japan's Lost Decade has grown to what may become a lost quarter century. Just as the country was beginning to emerge from the troubles of the 1990s and early 2000s, it was buffeted by the most recent liquidity shock, a crisis we turn to in Chapter 5, "The Great Recession."

Endnotes

1. For more details on how this period may be interpreted as the aftermath of a liquidity shock, please see George Chacko and Carolyn L. Evans (2011) "Japan's Lost Decade as a Liquidity-Shock Induced Downturn." Working Paper.

2. In the direct feedback mechanism, bank sales of assets with very low liquidity lead to further declines in the prices of those assets. In addition, there is "propagation" to other markets throughout the economy. With the dramatic drop in prices in the market for assets with very low liquidity, banks turn to selling somewhat more liquid assets, which leads to drops in prices in these other markets. Rounds of selling move through a wide range of markets, as banks shift from market to market searching for ways in which to take the least losses on their sales.

3. Peek and Rosengren write, "A bank must classify a loan as nonperforming when the borrower has failed to make interest payments for more than three months, the loan is restructured, or the firm declares bankruptcy." Joe Peek and Eric S. Rosengren (2005) "Unnatural Selection: Perverse Incentives and the Misallocation of Credit in Japan." *The American Economic Review* 95(4): 1144-1166.

4. Joe Peek and Eric S. Rosengren (2005) "Unnatural Selection: Perverse Incentives and the Misallocation of Credit in Japan." *The American Economic Review* 95(4): 1144-1166. See page 1150, footnote 5.

5. As noted in the previous chapter, the yield is essentially the rate of return that investors receive by buying a particular instrument. It moves in the opposite direction of the price of the asset. If an investor is willing to accept a low yield on an asset, it means that she intrinsically values that asset more than another asset with a higher yield. An increase in the yield is equivalent to a decline in its price, while a decrease in the yield is like a rise in its price.

6. There are also "zombie banks," banks that in reality are troubled, or even dead, but that mask their troubles during some time. We'll talk more about those in Chapter 6, "Conclusion."

7. Okina et al (2001) have pinned down the "bubble period" to between 1987 and 1990. They also point to "self-confidence in Japan" as one of the factors feeding the bubble. Kunio Okina, Masaaki Shirakawa, and Shigenori Shiratsuka (2001) "The asset price bubble and monetary policy: experience of Japan's economy in the late 1980s and its lessons." *Monetary and Economic Studies* 19 (S-1), Institute for Monetary and Economic Studies, Bank of Japan, pp. 395-450.

8. Thomas R. Zengage and C. Tait Ratcliffe (1988) *The Japanese Century: Challenge and Response*. Hong Kong: Longman Group (Far East) Ltd., p. ix.

9. Clyde V. Prestowitz, Jr. (1988) *Trading Places: How We Allowed Japan to Take the Lead*. New York: Basic Books, Inc., p. 310.

10. Clyde V. Prestowitz, Jr. (1988) *Trading Places: How We Allowed Japan to Take the Lead*. New York: Basic Books, Inc., p. 309.

11. Thomas Pepper, Merit E. Janow, and Jimmy W. Wheeler (1985) *The Competition: Dealing with Japan*. New York: Praeger Publishers; Eisuke Sakakibara (1993) *Beyond Capitalism: The Japanese Model of Market Economics*. Lanham, Maryland: University Press of America, Economic Strategy Institute.

12. See Kunio Okina, Masaaki Shirakawa, and Shigenori Shiratsuka (2001) "The asset price bubble and monetary policy: experience of Japan's economy in the late 1980s and its lessons." *Monetary and Economic Studies* 19 (S-1), Institute for Monetary and Economic Studies, Bank of Japan, pp. 395-450.

13. Hoshi and Kashyap provide a concise overview of these changes, highlighting a few developments as particularly important. See Takeo Hoshi and Anil Kashyap (2000) "The Japanese Banking Crisis: Where Did It Come From and How Will It End?" in NBER Macroeconomics Annual 1999, Volume 14, Eds. Ben S. Bernanke and Julio J. Rotemberg, MIT, pp. 129-212, http://www.nber.org/chapters/c11047.

14. There were also some changes occurring in terms of the rules faced by banks, but these occurred much more slowly and did not fully emerge until the "Big Bang" of the late 1990s. See Takeo Hoshi and Anil Kashyap (2000) "The Japanese Banking Crisis: Where Did It Come From and How Will It End?" in NBER Macroeconomics Annual 1999, Volume 14, Eds. Ben S. Bernanke and Julio J. Rotemberg, MIT, pp. 129-212, http://www.nber.org/chapters/c11047.

15. See Kunio Okina, Masaaki Shirakawa, and Shigenori Shiratsuka (2001) "The asset price bubble and monetary policy: experience of Japan's economy in the late 1980s and its lessons." *Monetary and Economic Studies* 19 (S-1), Institute for Monetary and Economic Studies, Bank of Japan, pp. 395-450.

16. Takeo Hoshi and Anil Kashyap (2000) "The Japanese Banking Crisis: Where Did It Come From and How Will It End?" in NBER Macroeconomics Annual 1999, Volume 14, Eds. Ben S. Bernanke and Julio J. Rotemberg, MIT, pp. 129-212, http://www.nber.org/chapters/c11047.

17. From Hoshi and Kahsyap (2000) "The Japanese Banking Crisis: Where Did It Come From and How Will It End?" in *NBER Macroeconomics Annual* 1999, Volume 14, Eds. Ben S. Bernanke and Julio J. Rotemberg, MIT, pp. 129-212, http://www.nber.org/chapters/c11047, the original source of this figure: "These data are taken from the Bank of Japan Economic Statistics Monthly. The small firms here are defined to be those that are not large according to the Bank of Japan definition: large firms are those firms which have more than ¥100 million in equity and more than 300 regular employees. The definition of small firms here roughly corresponds to that in the other tables in this paper." This explanation is on page 163 of their paper.

18. Kunio Okina and Shigenori Shiratsuka (2002) "Asset price bubbles, price stability and monetary policy: Japan's experience." *Monetary and Economic Studies* 20 (3), Institute for Monetary and Economic Studies, Bank of Japan, pp. 35-76.

19. Kunio Okina, Masaaki Shirakawa, and Shigenori Shiratsuka (2001) "The asset price bubble and monetary policy: experience of Japan's economy in the late 1980s and its lessons." *Monetary and Economic Studies* 19 (S-1), Institute for Monetary and Economic Studies, Bank of Japan, pp. 395-450.

20. Kunio Okina, Masaaki Shirakawa, and Shigenori Shiratsuka (2001): "The asset price bubble and monetary policy: experience of Japan's economy in the late 1980s and its lessons." *Monetary and Economic Studies* 19 (S-1), Institute for Monetary and Economic Studies, Bank of Japan, pp. 395-450.

21. Akihiro Kanaya and David Woo (2000) "The Japanese Banking Crisis of the 1990s: Sources and Lessons." International Monetary Fund Monetary and Exchange Affairs Department WP/OO/7.

22. Masaaki Shirakawa "Uniqueness or similarity? Japan's post-bubble experience in monetary policy studies," Keynote address by Masaaki Shirakawa, Governor of the Bank of Japan, at the Second International Journal of Central Banking (IJCB) Fall Conference, Tokyo, 16 September 2010, http://www.bis.org/review/r100920b.pdf?frames=0.

23. Hiroshi Nakaso (2001) "The financial crisis in Japan during the 1990s: how the Bank of Japan responded and the lessons learnt." BIS Papers No 6, Bank for International Settlements, Monetary and Economic Department.

24. Takeo Hoshi and Anil K. Kashyap (2010) "Will the U.S. bank recapitalization succeed? Eight lessons from Japan." *Journal of Financial Economics* 97(3) 398-417; Akihiro Kanaya and David Woo (2000) "The Japanese Banking Crisis of the 1990s: Sources and Lessons." International Monetary Fund Monetary and Exchange Affairs Department WP/OO/7; Hiroshi Nakaso (2001) "The financial crisis in Japan during the 1990s: how the Bank of Japan responded and the lessons learnt." BIS Papers No 6, Bank for International Settlements, Monetary and Economic Department.

25. Hiroshi Nakaso (2001) "The financial crisis in Japan during the 1990s: how the Bank of Japan responded and the lessons learnt." BIS Papers No 6, Bank for International Settlements, Monetary and Economic Department.

26. Takeo Hoshi and Anil K. Kashyap (2010) "Will the U.S. bank recapitalization succeed? Eight lessons from Japan." *Journal of Financial Economics* 97(3) 398-417; and Takatoshi Ito and Kimie Harada (2005) "Japan Premium and Stock Prices: Two Mirrors of Japanese Banking Crises." *International Journal of Finance and Economics* 10: 195-211.

27. http://www.boj.or.jp/en/announcements/press/danwa/dan9711e.htm/. "Joint Statement by the Minister of Finance and the Governor of the Bank of Japan" (tentative translation), November 26, 1997. Ministry of Finance, Bank of Japan. (Web page: Bank of Japan > Announcements > Speeches and Statements > Statements > JOINT STATEMENT by the Minister of Finance and the Governor of the Bank of Japan (tentative translation)). Accessed March 21, 2011.

28. Japan Securities and Exchange Surveillance Commission, Annual Report, Outline of Activities July 1997-June 1998, Chapter 7: Inspections of Financial Institutions by the Financial Supervisory Agency (Minister of Finance), http://www.fsa.go.jp/sesc/english/reports/reports.htm.

29. Yasuo Matsushita (1997) "Recent Financial and Economic Conditions in Japan." Speeches and Statements, Bank of Japan Web site, http://www.boj.or.jp/en/announcements/press/koen_1997/ko9802a.htm/, accessed February 4, 2011.

30. Takeo Hoshi and Anil K. Kashyap (2010) "Will the U.S. bank recapitalization succeed? Eight lessons from Japan." *Journal of Financial Economics* 97(3) 398-417.

31. Hiroshi Nakaso (2001) "The financial crisis in Japan during the 1990s: how the Bank of Japan responded and the lessons learnt." BIS Papers No 6, Bank for International Settlements, Monetary and Economic Department.

32. Takeo Hoshi and Anil K. Kashyap (2010) "Will the U.S. bank recapitalization succeed? Eight lessons from Japan." *Journal of Financial Economics* 97(3) 398-417.

33. Hoshi and Kahsyap (2010) also make the point that in December 1997, the government changed the rules governing banks reporting on assets. It allowed banks to choose either market or book value for bank holdings of both stocks and real estate assets. By choosing the value that provided the most favorable view of their books, banks may have found another way to hide underlying financial weakness. See Takeo Hoshi and Anil K. Kashyap (2010) "Will the U.S. bank recapitalization succeed? Eight lessons from Japan." *Journal of Financial Economics* 97(3) 398-417.

34. These numbers incorporate redefinitions in 1997 and 1998. International Monetary Fund (2001), "Japan: 2001 Article IV Consultation-Staff Report; Staff Statement; and Public Information Notice on the Executive Board Discussion." IMF Country Report No. 01/144, August 2001.

35. This peak occurred just around the time when the Financial Services Agency (FSA) completed its special inspections of major banks, which took place between October and March 2002. Also see Takeo Hoshi and Anil K. Kashyap (2010) "Will the U.S. bank recapitalization succeed? Eight lessons from Japan." *Journal of Financial Economics* 97(3) 398-417.

36. According to the FSA, "The aim of the special inspections is to ensure an appropriate classification of borrowers as well as sufficient level of write-offs and provisioning on a timely basis, reflecting the borrowers' business conditions and market signals against them." This inspection found that

almost half the borrowers needed to be downgraded. "Results of the Special Inspections on Major Banks." http://www.fsa.go.jp/news/newse/e20020412-1.html, accessed February 4, 2011.

37. Takeo Hoshi and Anil Kashyap (2000) "The Japanese Banking Crisis: Where Did It Come From and How Will It End?" in NBER Macroeconomics Annual 1999, Volume 14, Eds. Ben S. Bernanke and Julio J. Rotemberg, MIT, pp. 129-212, http://www.nber.org/chapters/c11047. 1980 to 1992 are the dates provided by Hoshi and Kashyap in their analysis. See Table 16, p. 181, in their paper.

38. Akihiro Kanaya and David Woo (2000) "The Japanese Banking Crisis of the 1990s: Sources and Lessons." International Monetary Fund Monetary and Exchange Affairs Department WP/OO/7, p. 43.

39. Yuzo Honda (2002) "The effects of the Basle accord on bank credit: the case of Japan." *Applied Economics* 34: 1233-1239.

40. See Joe Peek and Eric S. Rosengren (2005) "Unnatural Selection: Perverse Incentives and the Misallocation of Credit in Japan." *The American Economic Review* 95(4): 1144-1166.

41. Takeo Hoshi and Anil K. Kashyap (2010) "Will the U.S. bank recapitalization succeed? Eight lessons from Japan." *Journal of Financial Economics* 97(3) 398-417.

42. Akihiro Kanaya and David Woo (2000) "The Japanese Banking Crisis of the 1990s: Sources and Lessons." International Monetary Fund Monetary and Exchange Affairs Department WP/OO/7 and Hiroshi Nakaso (2001) "The financial crisis in Japan during the 1990s: how the Bank of Japan responded and the lessons learnt." BIS Papers No 6, Bank for International Settlements, Monetary and Economic Department.

43. Akihiro Kanaya and David Woo (2000) "The Japanese Banking Crisis of the 1990s: Sources and Lessons." International Monetary Fund Monetary and Exchange Affairs Department WP/OO/7.

44. For example, see Takeo Hoshi and Anil K. Kashyap (2010) "Will the U.S. bank recapitalization succeed? Eight lessons from Japan." *Journal of Financial Economics* 97(3) 398-417; Anil Kashyap (2002) "Sorting Out Japan's Financial Crisis." *Economic Perspectives* 26(Q4) Federal Reserve Bank of Chicago, pp. 42–256; Hiroshi Nakaso (2001) "The financial crisis in

Japan during the 1990s: how the Bank of Japan responded and the lessons learnt." BIS Papers No 6, Bank for International Settlements, Monetary and Economic Department; and Akihiro Kanaya and David Woo (2000) "The Japanese Banking Crisis of the 1990s: Sources and Lessons." International Monetary Fund Monetary and Exchange Affairs Department WP/OO/7.

45. Akihiro Kanaya and David Woo (2000) "The Japanese Banking Crisis of the 1990s: Sources and Lessons." International Monetary Fund Monetary and Exchange Affairs Department WP/OO/7.

46. Domestic credit to private sector refers to financial resources provided to the private sector, such as through loans, purchases of nonequity securities, and trade credits and other accounts receivable, that establish a claim for repayment. For some countries these claims include credit to public enterprises.

47. Joe Peek and Eric S. Rosengren (2005) "Unnatural Selection: Perverse Incentives and the Misallocation of Credit in Japan." *The American Economic Review* 95(4): 1144-1166.

48. In addition to banks revolving loans to firms, the government conducted a number of recapitalization initiatives over this time period. Thus, for example, the leap in the index (signifying a more accommodative attitude) in 1998 may reflect the government's Financial Function Stabilization Act and accompanying injection of bank capital.

49. Koo, in other work, also compares Japan's crisis to recent events in the United States. Richard C. Koo (2010) "U.S. Economy in Balance Sheet Recession: What the U.S. Can Learn from Japan's Experience in 1990–2005." Nomura Research Institute.

50. Masaaki Shirakawa "Uniqueness or similarity? Japan's post-bubble experience in monetary policy studies," Keynote address by Masaaki Shirakawa, Governor of the Bank of Japan, at the Second International Journal of Central Banking (IJCB) Fall Conference, Tokyo, 16 September 2010, http://www.bis.org/review/r100920b.pdf?frames=0.

References

Chacko, George and Evans, Carolyn L. 2011. "Japan's Lost Decade as a Liquidity-Shock Induced Downturn." Working Paper.

Honda, Yuzo. 2002. "The effects of the Basle accord on bank credit: the case of Japan." *Applied Economics* 34: 1233-1239.

Hoshi, Takeo and Anil Kashyap. 2000. "The Japanese Banking Crisis: Where Did It Come From and How Will It End?" in NBER Macroeconomics Annual 1999, Volume 14, Eds. Ben S. Bernanke and Julio J. Rotemberg, MIT, pp. 129-212, http://www.nber.org/chapters/c11047.

Hoshi, Takeo and Anil K. Kashyap. 2010. "Will the U.S. bank recapitalization succeed? Eight lessons from Japan." *Journal of Financial Economics* 97(3) 398-417, doi:10.1016/j.jfineco.2010.02.005.

International Monetary Fund. 2001. "Japan: 2001 Article IV Consultation-Staff Report; Staff Statement; and Public Information Notice on the Executive Board Discussion." IMF Country Report No. 01/144, August 2001.

Ito, Takatoshi and Kimie Harada. 2005. "Japan Premium and Stock Prices: Two Mirrors of Japanese Banking Crises." *International Journal of Finance and Economics* 10: 195-211.

Japan Securities and Exchange Surveillance Commission. Annual Report. Outline of Activities July 1997-June 1998. Chapter 7: Inspections of Financial Institutions by the Financial Supervisory Agency (Minister of Finance) http://www.fsa.go.jp/sesc/english/reports/reports.htm.

Kanaya, Akihiro and David Woo. 2000. "The Japanese Banking Crisis of the 1990s: Sources and Lessons." International Monetary Fund Monetary and Exchange Affairs Department WP/OO/7.

Kashyap, Anil. 2002. "Sorting Out Japan's Financial Crisis." *Economic Perspectives* 26(Q4) Federal Reserve Bank of Chicago, pp. 42–256.

Koo, Richard. 2003. *Balance Sheet Recession: Japan's Struggle with Uncharted Economics and Its Global Implications*. Singapore: John Wiley & Sons (Asia) Pte Ltd.

Koo, Richard C. 2010. "U.S. Economy in Balance Sheet Recession: What the U.S. Can Learn from Japan's Experience in 1990–2005." Nomura Research Institute.

Montgomery, Heather. 2007. "The effectiveness of bank recapitalization in Japan." *International Journal of Banking and Finance* 5(1) 113-134.

Nakaso, Hiroshi. 2001. "The financial crisis in Japan during the 1990s: how the Bank of Japan responded and the lessons learnt." BIS Papers No 6, Bank for International Settlements, Monetary and Economic Department.

Okina, Kunio, Masaaki Shirakawa, and Shigenori Shiratsuka. 2001. "The asset price bubble and monetary policy: experience of Japan's economy in the late 1980s and its lessons." *Monetary and Economic Studies*, 19 (S-1), Institute for Monetary and Economic Studies, Bank of Japan, pp. 395-450.

Okina, Kunio and Shigenori Shiratsuka. 2002. "Asset price bubbles, price stability and monetary policy: Japan's experience." Monetary and Economic Studies, 20 (3), Institute for Monetary and Economic Studies, Bank of Japan, pp. 35-76.

Peek, Joe and Eric S. Rosengren. 2005. "Unnatural Selection: Perverse Incentives and the Misallocation of Credit in Japan." *The American Economic Review* 95(4): 1144-1166.

Pepper, Thomas. Merit E. Janow, and Jimmy W. Wheeler. 1985. *The Competition: Dealing with Japan*. New York: Praeger Publishers.

Prestowitz, Clyde V., Jr. 1988. *Trading Places: How We Allowed Japan to Take the Lead*. New York: Basic Books, Inc.

Sakakibara, Eisuke. 1993. *Beyond Capitalism: The Japanese Model of Market Economics*. Lanham, Maryland: University Press of America, Inc. Economic Strategy Institute.

Shirakawa, Masaaki. "Uniqueness or similarity? Japan's post-bubble experience in monetary policy studies," Keynote address by Masaaki Shirakawa, Governor of the Bank of Japan, at the Second International Journal of Central Banking (IJCB) Fall Conference, Tokyo, 16 September 2010. http://www.bis.org/review/r100920b.pdf?frames=0.

Woo, David. 2003. "In Search of 'Capital Crunch': Supply Factors behind the Credit Slowdown in Japan." *Journal of Money, Credit and Banking* 35(6, Part 1): 1019-1038.

Zengage, Thomas R. and C. Tait Ratcliffe. 1988. *The Japanese Century: Challenge and Response*. Hong Kong: Longman Group (Far East) Ltd.

chapter 5

The Great Recession

As the most recent episode of a liquidity crisis, the U.S. Great Recession provides another ready example to illustrate our argument.[1] Between 2008 and 2009, the United States experienced the worst economic downturn since the Great Depression. Stock and home prices plunged, wiping out trillions of dollars of wealth in a short period of time. As we write this in early 2011, there have been signs of recovery, but unemployment levels (traditionally a lagging indicator) remained around 10% at the end of 2010, more than double late-2006 levels of around 4% to 5%.

5.1 The Stages of a Liquidity Shock— Same Applies Now as with the Great Depression

Our discussion of the U.S. Great Recession is structured as in the previous two chapters. To briefly review the framework, Figure 5.1 again sets out the stages of a liquidity shock followed by a recession. There is first *an initial trigger*. With the Great Depression, we observed that it was the combination of crashes in real estate, stocks, and worldwide commodity prices, while for Japan, we identified the plunge in real estate. For the case of the U.S. Great Recession, we will again identify a trigger, which is generally a sudden drop in the fundamental value of some asset.

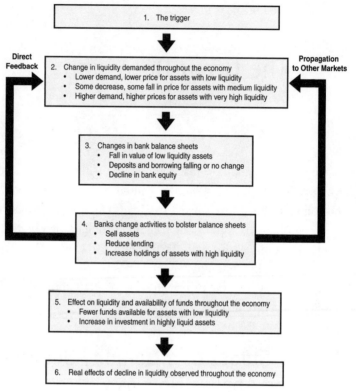

Figure 5.1 *The stages of a liquidity shock*

This trigger in turn leads to a *change in the liquidity demanded throughout the economy*. Investors become concerned that they will be unable to buy or sell an asset at a particular point in time at a favorable rate, and therefore turn away from assets for which that ability to buy or sell quickly may be in jeopardy, with a residential home being a classic example. With a liquidity shock, residential real estate would be something that would become much less attractive to potential investors. Thus, with a liquidity shock, prices of assets with low liquidity should fall. In contrast, investors become eager to hold highly liquid assets, so the prices of highly liquid assets should rise.

The next stage of the liquidity shock occurs as the change in liquidity needs throughout the economy feeds through to *changes in bank balance sheets*. Once the liquidity shock hits and the prices of the low liquidity assets fall, there is a fall in the value of the left-hand side of a bank's balance sheet tied up in these low liquidity assets. The main entry on the right-hand (liabilities) side of the balance sheet—deposits—may fall a bit, but by much less than the decline in assets. At the same time, and dictated by the fact that the two sides of the balance sheet must always be equal, the decline in the value of its assets means that a bank's equity must also fall (which would be reflected as a fall in the share price of a publicly traded bank).

Subsequently, banks must *change activities to bolster their balance sheets*. With the decline in equity, the bank's ratio of equity to assets has also fallen. The bank could now shift away from low liquidity assets, for instance by calling in loans and/or reining in new lending. It will likely also shift toward holding very liquid assets, such as investing more in cash and government bonds. It wants to hold very liquid assets because they are both easy to trade and of low risk. As we noted earlier, there are also two ways in which changes in bank activities feed back into prices in financial markets—directly and via propagation to other markets.[2]

Next (Stage 5 in Figure 5.1), we need to bring in the fact that the changes by banks affect firms and individuals throughout the economy, as *fewer funds become available for assets with low liquidity, and there is increased investment in highly liquid assets*. Then, as the final stage of the liquidity shock, the real effects of the change in availability of funds hit the broader economy. The *real effects of the decline in liquidity will be observed throughout the economy*, which may be observed via the macroeconomic indicators commonly reported. At this point, the economy is in a recession that at its surface may appear similar to other recessions not induced by a liquidity shock.

5.2 Recognizing a Liquidity Shock—Interpreting the Data

To show how a liquidity shock may manifest itself, we again look to real, measurable indicators in the data that show us how and whether a particular economic crisis is related to liquidity. In this section, we set out exactly how we do so for the U.S. Great Recession. Our discussion for this event is for the most part similar to our coverage in the previous two chapters. However, this case differs a bit due to the systemic changes that occurred in the U.S. financial system prior to the triggering event that we identify. We provide more extensive discussion in the section "Setting the Stage for the Trigger—the Background to the Great Recession" later in the chapter, but for now we note that we again look mainly to data on banks, but these data are then supplemented by information on events in the alternative banking system that developed in the United States prior to the liquidity crisis.

The initial event in these liquidity-shock induced crises is a trigger (see Table 5.1). As with our previous two cases, the trigger for the case of the U.S. Great Recession is linked to changes in prices in real estate. For this most recent case, however, the process was a bit more subtle. Here, a flattening out of prices, together with other factors, rather than a steep fall, kicked off the liquidity crisis. Thus, we present information on both real and nominal housing prices, using the widely cited Case-Shiller Index, which carefully controls for possible differences across individual homes sold. An increase in default rates was also important, so we provide information on delinquency rates on loans.

Table 5.1   *The Trigger*

Topic	Evidence
Real estate market slackening	Nominal and real housing price indices
	Case-Shiller Index
Increase in default rates	Delinquency rates on loans

During the initial phases of the liquidity shock, we expect the decline in demand for assets with low liquidity to lead to lower prices for such assets (see Table 5.2). (To recall why, please see Figure 3.3.) Here, we examine nominal and real housing prices, using the Case-Shiller Index, which controls for changes in the quality of housing, since a house is a relatively less liquid asset. To sell a residence, a seller must be matched with a buyer interested in that particular house. The two parties must then agree on a price and complete the transaction. For someone interested in an asset that can be converted into cash quickly, a house is clearly not an asset that would be of much use.

Table 5.2   *Change in Liquidity Demanded Throughout the Economy*

Topic	Evidence
Decrease in Demand for Assets with Low Liquidity → Fall in Price of Low Liquidity Assets	
Residential real estate	Nominal and real housing price indices (Case-Shiller Index)
Increase in Demand for High Liquidity Assets → Increase in Price of High Liquidity Assets	
Short-term federal government debt	Yields on U.S. Treasury bills
Increase in Demand for High Versus Low Liquidity Assets → Increase in Price of High Liquidity Assets Relative to Price of Low Liquidity Assets	
Long-term versus short-term government debt	Yields on one-year versus 20-year U.S. Treasury securities
Government bonds relative to corporate bonds	Risk premium on lending (spread between prime rate and short-term government securities)

Conversely, prices of assets with very high liquidity would be expected to rise, so we also consider the prices of assets with very high liquidity. U.S. Treasury bills represent borrowing by the U.S. federal government. These bonds are highly liquid—they can easily be converted into cash at a predictable price.

Finally, we explore changes in the prices of assets with very high liquidity relative to the prices of assets with somewhat lower liquidity. The first comparison that we make is between yields on 20-year and yields on one-year Treasury bills. Here, the one-year bill is considered the more liquid of the two; since it will be paid off soon anyway, others are happy to purchase it at a predictable price. Thus, when we see a bigger fall in the yield on the one-year than in the yield on the 20-year, it means that the yield on the less liquid (20-year) has increased relative to the yield on the more liquid (one-year). Recalling that yields move in the opposite direction of prices, this in turn means that the price of the less liquid 20-year has fallen relative to the price on the more liquid one-year—liquidity has become more valuable.[3]

We also examine data on *spreads,* the difference between the rates on two different securities. A larger spread implies that the two different securities are viewed as being very different—with one more desirable than the other. A small spread means that the two securities are priced closely to each other. We examine the spread between the rate on short-term corporate borrowing and the rate on short-term government securities. Here, an increase in the spread is what we would expect when liquidity becomes more coveted, since it means that the rate on the less liquid corporate borrowing has increased relative to the rate on the liquid short-term government security. Another way to think about it is as meaning that the prices of the less liquid corporate bonds are falling relative to the price on the very liquid short-term government securities. An increase in the spread is what would be predicted in the aftermath of a liquidity shock.

Next, we examine changes in bank balance sheets to see whether the changes that we would expect to occur in a liquidity crisis happened in the case of the U.S. Great Recession (see Table 5.3). We would expect to see a fall in the value of bank assets with low liquidity, namely loans; bank deposits either falling or changing little; and a decline in bank equity. Thus, we look directly at some of these main categories of bank balance sheets—assets with low liquidity (loans), banks' main liability (deposits), and the value of a bank's equity (stockholders' equity). We also provide information on the spread between financial and nonfinancial commercial paper, which provides some indication of the condition of the financial sector versus that of the nonfinancial sector.

Table 5.3   *Changes in Bank Balance Sheets*

Topic	Evidence
Fall in Value of Bank Assets with Low Liquidity	
Bank loans	Total bank assets
	Bank credit
	Bank loans, total and by type of borrower
Bank Deposits Falling or No Change	
Bank deposits	Bank deposits
Decline in Bank Equity	
Bank equity	Bank equity capital
Overall Bank Viability	
Financial sector condition	Spread between financial and nonfinancial commercial paper

Faced with changes in the balance sheet discussed previously, a bank must take action to shore up its position (see Table 5.4). One effective action could be to shift away from low liquidity assets, and we look to data on bank holdings of low liquidity assets to see whether they decline, examining the value of total loans. We also provide a breakdown across types of loans to examine whether differential trends by type of lending may provide some information as to the value placed on liquidity. As another indicator, we examine bank holdings of assets with very high liquidity. Here, we focus on the most liquid of assets—cash, which is the most liquid by its very nature—as well as government securities, which are also very liquid since they are easy to sell at a predictable price at any point in time. Finally, we have information on the ratio of banks' highly liquid reserves—cash and deposits with the Central Bank—to their assets that are claims on (i.e., loans to) the private sector and others. If this ratio is high, it suggests that banks are keeping their assets as liquid as possible, rather than lending them out in ways that might reduce their liquidity.

Table 5.4   *Banks Change Activities to Bolster Balance Sheet*

Topic	Evidence
Reduce Lending and/or Sell Assets with Low Liquidity	
Holdings of assets with low liquidity	Loans, total and by type
Increase in Holdings of Assets with High Liquidity	
Holdings of assets with very high liquidity	Bank cash holdings Bank holdings of central government securities
Increase Holdings of High Liquidity Relative to Low Liquidity Assets	
Fraction of high liquidity relative to low liquidity assets	Bank liquid reserves to bank assets ratio (percent)

The changes in bank behavior induced by the liquidity shock in turn impact the availability of funds throughout the economy (see Table 5.5). Fewer funds become available for assets with low liquidity. We examine both consumer credit and mortgage debt outstanding as indicators of the availability of credit to households. A decline in such lending would imply net tightening of credit to this group. As for the corporate sector, we provide information on credit market borrowing by the business sector, as well as results from a senior loan

officer opinion survey. Finally, as an indicator of overall credit availability we consider total domestic credit to the private sector. This
should tell us generally how available credit is within the economy.

Table 5.5   *Effect on Liquidity and Availability of Funds Throughout
the Economy*

Topic	Evidence
General Decline in Availability of Funds for Assets with Low Liquidity	
Lending to households	Consumer credit outstanding
Lending to households	Mortgage debt outstanding
Availability of funds to households	Senior loan officer opinion survey
Availability of funds to corporate sector	Credit market borrowing by business sector
Availability of funds to corporate sector	Senior loan officer opinion survey
Availability of Credit to Overall Economy	
General availability of credit	Domestic credit to the private sector

Finally, we expect the impact of the shrinking of credit to be felt
throughout the entire economy (see Table 5.6). The shock moves
"from Wall Street to Main Street," or from the financial sector to the
general economy. To illustrate this stage of the crisis, we again focus
especially on real estate and construction—sectors that generally
require credit to function but that need this credit for assets (build-
ings, homes, etc.) with relatively low liquidity. New housing starts tell
us about whether new activity is being undertaken, which would have
required financing to get started, and we also look at new building
permits for the same reason. In addition, we discuss the availability of
funds to small businesses. To learn about the state of the broader
economy, we consider Gross Domestic Product (GDP), an index of
industrial production, the unemployment rate, and trends in new job
openings. GDP is the broadest measure of all for economic activity
taking place in a country, while the unemployment rate and new job

openings tell us about jobs. We also examine trends in prices. These measures, taken together, provide a good idea of the overall level of economic activity in the country after the liquidity shock hit.

Table 5.6 *Real Effects of Decline in Liquidity Observed Throughout the Economy*

Topic	Evidence
Decline in Activity in Sectors Requiring Funding, but Considered to Have Relatively Low Liquidity	
Activity in real estate	New housing starts
	New building permits
Availability of funds to small businesses	Survey of small businesses
Overall Economic Activity	
Gross Domestic Product (GDP)	Real GDP
Aggregate Economic Activity	Industrial Production Index
Overall Price Trends	
Inflation and deflation	Consumer Price Index
Employment and Unemployment	
Unemployment rate	Unemployment and underemployment rates
Employment opportunities	New job openings and hirings
Severity and longevity of unemployment	Long-term unemployment and discouraged workers

5.3 Setting the Stage for the Trigger— the Background to the Great Recession

As with the Great Depression and Japan's Lost Decade, the period preceding the Great Recession was one of boom and expansion. For the Great Depression, we described the takeoff in stocks and land prices. For the case of Japan, we observed a "bubble" in stocks and in land, particularly in land in large cities. For the U.S. Great Recession, we also observed a takeoff in housing prices, a trend that occurred around the country.

Between 2001 and mid-2006, U.S. housing prices grew at a much faster pace than historical trends, as shown in Figure 5.2. Figure 5.3 shows another indicator of home prices—the Case-Shiller Price Index, which carefully controls for possible differences across individual homes sold. Figure 5.3 shows monthly figures for composites of 10 large metro areas and 20 large metro areas. We see that this index began to escalate in value beginning in the early 2000s. As shown, this increase shows up looking at both the 10-metro area (including areas such as New York, Los Angeles, Chicago, San Francisco, and Boston) and the broader 20-metro area composite, which adds areas such as Phoenix, Arizona, and Tampa, Florida, to the 10-area composite.

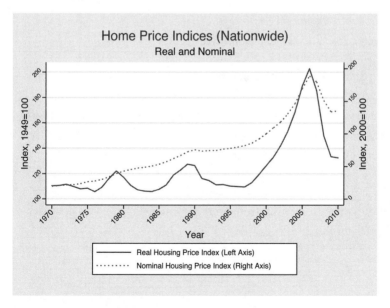

Source: Robert Shiller (http://www.econ.yale.edu/~shiller/data.htm)

Figure 5.2 *The boom in real estate*

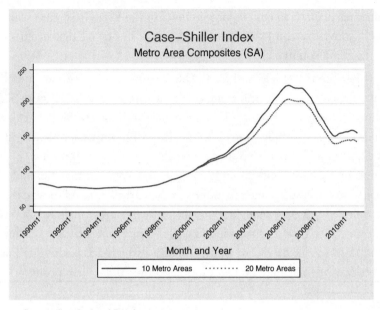

Source: Standard and Poor's

Figure 5.3 *Case-Shiller Index metro composites*

Interestingly, however, the real estate bubble was not experienced by every area of the country. Figure 5.4 shows the Case-Shiller indices for Las Vegas, Portland, Miami, and Cleveland. The explosion in prices was much more pronounced in Miami and Las Vegas than in Cleveland, for example. Thus, certain areas of the country experienced much more of a robust expansion in home prices than others. In any case, considering the nation as a whole (shown in Figure 5.5), the overall trend was tremendous growth in home prices between 2002 and 2006.

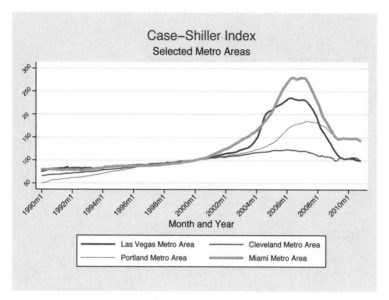

Source: Standard and Poor's
Seasonally adjusted

Figure 5.4 *Case-Shiller Index selected metro areas*

Again echoing the two earlier episodes covered in Chapter 3, "The Great Depression," and Chapter 4, "Japan's Lost Decade," contemporary observers did not recognize the emerging bubble. For example, in a 2006 report on housing prices in a number of countries, the Organization for Economic Cooperation and Development (OECD) concluded that home prices were "overvalued" (i.e., that prices exceeded their "fundamental" value) for the UK, Ireland, the Netherlands, and Spain. For the United States, however, the authors concluded that "there does not appear to be much of a case for overvaluation, at least at the national level."[4] A 2004 press release describing the most recent report from the Harvard Joint Center for Housing Studies noted that "looking ahead, the report finds reason to believe that residential investment will reach new heights again over the next ten years."[5]

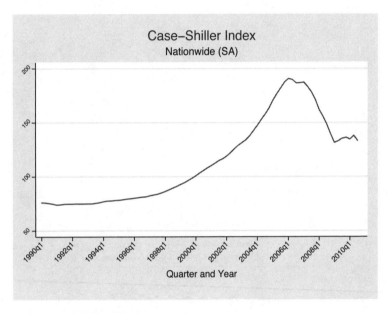

Source: Standard and Poor's

Figure 5.5   *Case-Shiller Index nationwide*

As for broad economic indicators, gross domestic product was expanding smartly starting in 2003 (shown in Figure 5.6). Inside the United States, policymakers apparently held bullish views on the economy. As one example, President George W. Bush, after meeting with his economic team in August 2005, noted that "The economy of the United States is strong, and the foundation for sustained growth is in place."[6] Indeed, around the world, the U.S. economy was viewed as a key component of global prosperity. For example, as late as July 2006 the International Monetary Fund (IMF), in its annual report on the U.S. economy, wrote, "The U.S. economy has remained a key engine of global growth, despite devastating hurricanes, a withdrawal of monetary stimulus, and high energy prices. Activity has remained robust, supported by strong productivity growth...."[7] Thus, observers around the world were optimistic about prospects for the U.S. economy and viewed growth in the years preceding the Great Recession as robust and sustainable.

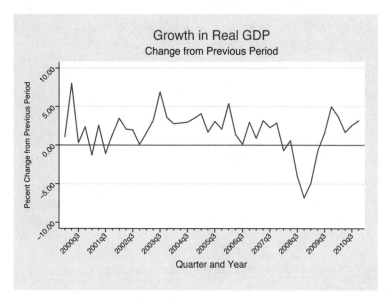

Source: U.S. Bureau of Economic Analysis
Seasonally adjusted annual rate

Figure 5.6 *GDP growth*

In Chapters 3 and 4, in looking back at the bubbles preceding both the U.S. Great Depression and Japan's Lost Decade, we observed that easy monetary policy and changes in the financial sector were factors supporting and contributing to the bubble. Such elements were also present as the bubble emerged in the United States.

Regarding monetary policy, Figure 5.7 shows the federal funds rate targeted by the U.S. Federal Reserve. This rate is a key instrument of U.S. monetary policy and determines the rate charged by banks to each other for overnight loans. Faced with signs of slowing growth in early 2001, the Fed reduced this target by 50 basis points, from 5.5% to 5% on March 20 of that year.[8] Further reductions came in April (-50 basis points), May (-50 basis points), June (-25 basis points), and August (-25 basis points). Then, when the country and the economy were jolted by the events of September 11, 2001, the Fed responded with a series of declines, with the target rate ending up at 1 3/4% by the end of 2001.

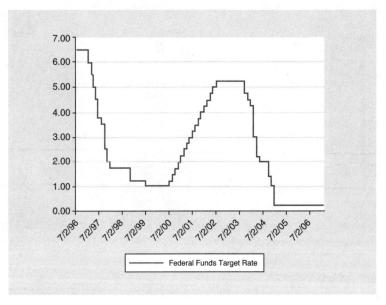

Source: Federal Reserve Bank of New York, http://www.newyorkfed.org/markets/omo/dmm/historical/fedfunds/index.cfm.

Figure 5.7   *Federal funds target rate*

Virtually none would argue with Fed Policy through the end of 2001. However, some critics have suggested that the series of reductions in the target rate undertaken in subsequent years constituted overly easy monetary policy and may have contributed to the bubble. At the time, recent events in Japan—the Lost Decade and ongoing deflation—would likely have been in the minds of policymakers.[9] As we discussed in Chapter 4, once a country enters a deflationary spiral, recovery becomes difficult, if not next to impossible. Thus, there were good reasons to continue an easy money policy. However, some have criticized the policy as being too loose and as an important causal factor behind the bubble. John Taylor, for example, argued that the federal funds rate during this period was lower than would have been dictated by historical experience. He concludes that "there is clearly evidence of monetary excesses during the period leading up to the housing boom."[10] Thus, as with the U.S. Great Depression and Japan's Lost Decade, easy monetary policy may have contributed to the emerging bubble in real estate.

Finally, and perhaps most saliently in the minds of the public, an important contributing factor was the changes in financial markets, financial instruments, and financial institutions that occurred during the period preceding the bursting of the bubble. To explain these changes, we need to refer again to the basic functions of banks. Banks take deposits from individuals and issue loans to borrowers. Banks also hold equity (i.e., bank capital). Banks are required, by law, to hold a certain amount of capital relative to their assets. This requirement is intended to reduce the risk that a bank will go under in the event that it faces a rush of depositors demanding the return of their funds.

This requirement to hold a certain amount of capital, however, means that it is harder for a bank to satisfy the demands of stockholders that they receive adequate returns on their stock holdings. More specifically, firms are often judged by their *return on equity* (ROE). This is the ratio of profits to equity (i.e., capital). The combination of the need to generate a reasonable return on equity, on the one hand, and the regulatory requirement to maintain a certain capital adequacy ratio (i.e., a minimum level of capital relative to risk-weighted assets), on the other, has a number of effects on banks' incentives.[11] Figure 5.8 roughly illustrates these incentives. First, to generate a higher ROE, a bank could either increase its profits or reduce its equity (top section of Figure 5.8). To increase profits, a bank could try increasing interest rates on loans to borrowers. However, borrowers could go to another bank or find another way to obtain funds (by issuing corporate bonds, for example). Thus, a bank must look for alternative ways to increase profits. As for equity, a bank's ability to reduce equity is limited by its need to maintain a certain level of capital to meet regulatory capital adequacy requirements.[12]

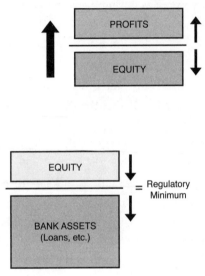

Figure 5.8 *Return on equity and capital adequacy ratios*

In light of this situation, a number of developments took place in financial markets. First, given the difficulties that banks faced in generating an attractive ROE, a range of alternative financial institutions arose that performed many of the functions of banks, but that were not deposit-taking institutions. We use the term *bank alternatives* to refer to these institutions.[13] Examples include finance companies such as GE Capital and CIT Group. Figure 5.9 shows a basic balance sheet for a bank alternative. The asset side of the balance sheet looks essentially like that of a bank—it makes loans to individuals and to firms. (One difference is that these loans are often held in the form of securitized pools of loans initiated by other institutions, a point that we return to in a moment.) The liabilities side of the balance sheet, however, is different from a traditional bank in one key way—a bank alternative does not take deposits directly from individuals. Rather, it funds itself via short-term debt that may take the form of money-market mutual funds, repurchase agreements, or other short-term debt. By foregoing deposits, bank alternatives are able to operate outside the regulatory framework for banks and thus are not required by regulation to maintain a certain capital adequacy ratio. Thus, they are able to hold a lower level of equity relative to assets, if they choose to do so. (Of course, such firms would still have an incentive to maintain a level of capital adequate for running a sustainable business.)[14] As a result, for a given value of profits, a bank alternative would be able to generate a higher ROE than would a traditional bank.

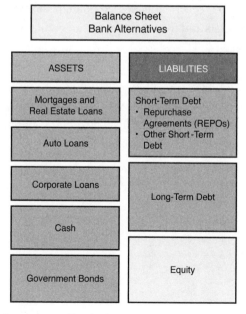

Figure 5.9   *Balance sheet of bank alternatives*

The second development in financial markets that took place was in the behavior of banks. Since banks are required by regulation to hold a certain amount of capital relative to their assets, the size of this capital base may be higher than it would otherwise be, which would tend to drag down its ROE. However, if a bank is able to sell a chunk of assets, it reduces the level of equity that it is required to hold (refer to Figure 5.8). This would serve to push up the bank's ROE. (The selling off of loans also meant that banks were getting rid of the risk associated with these loans, another attractive feature.) Thus, what banks often chose to do was to sell off their loans, often to the bank alternatives described previously.

Figure 5.10 provides some indication of growth in activities associated with the alternative banking sector. It shows total financial assets of finance companies, which are one of the institutions in the alternative banking sector. Finance companies make loans, but they do not take deposits and thus do not face the regulatory requirements that apply to banks. They make loans for things such as commercial and residential real estate, consumer auto purchases, and business receivables. After increasing gradually throughout the 1980s and most of the 1990s, the total financial assets in finance companies grew by 122% between 1998 and 2007. This is just one variety of bank alternative that emerged during the 1990s.

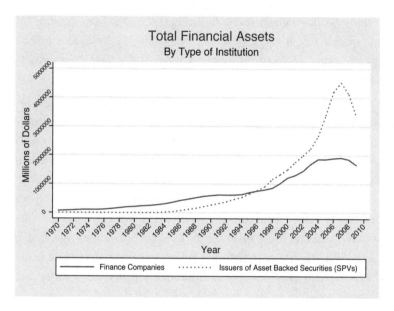

Source: U.S. Flow of Funds

Figure 5.10 *Growth in bank alternatives*

Figure 5.10 also provides information on issuers of asset-backed securities. These are *special purpose vehicles* or SPVs that are not really firms but exist as legal entities to hold assets that were originally held by other firms, often banks. The SPVs buy assets, which may be student loans, home mortgages, auto loans, or other types of loans, and then pool them together and issue bonds backed by the assets. (This process is called *securitization*.)[15] They are one way in which banks are able to get assets, such as mortgages, off their balance sheets. By removing these assets from their balance sheets, they are able to reduce the amount of capital that they are required by regulation to hold, which in turn helps them improve their return on equity (ROE), as discussed previously. Figure 5.10 shows that the total financial assets held by SPVs skyrocketed from the late 1990s to 2007. This growth was particularly marked during the mid-2000s, when it more than doubled in just four years before peaking in 2007. This provides one additional piece of information about the growth in activities in the alternative banking sector.

Returning to our discussion of the bubble in housing prices described earlier, the emergence of an alternative set of institutions that performed many of the functions of banks, but that were not banks per se, allowed a great deal of capital to flow into the housing markets during the bubble period, in some cases with banks acting as conduits for the flow of loans from individual borrowers to the bank alternatives which held the loans, often in securitized form. More broadly speaking, these changes in financial institutions and markets changed the traditional relationship between assets and bank capital, where the extent of lending is limited by banks' need to maintain mandatory capital to asset ratios.

With this flood of money into the housing market came an easing of lending standards, as banks and other mortgage originators realized that they would be able to offload loans (and therefore risk) via the alternative banking system. Thus, the bubble period saw a mushrooming of nontraditional housing loans such as liar loans where no proof of income is necessary, and NINJA loans where individuals with No Income, No Job, and No Assets can qualify.[16] A March 2007 Credit Suisse report noted, based on the opinion of a private builder, that "in the past nine months anybody with a pulse that was interested in buying a home was able to get financing."[17] Indeed, the fraction of mortgages for current purchases going to subprime mortgages went from 6% in 2002 to 20% in 2006. During that same time period, the fraction in prime (both conforming and jumbo) fell from 81% to 57%.[18] One analyst calculated that in the few years prior to 2007, particularly easy subprime lending likely led to an extra 200,000 homes purchased per year, which was about 10% to 15% of total demand for new homes. Any change in the availability of subprime loans or lending standards would mean that home sales and prices could fall more than if lending standards did not change.[19]

A final important feature of the alternative banking system was the fact that the road between the initial provider of funds and the ultimate borrower of funds was often long and with many twists and turns. As two researchers at the Federal Reserve Bank of New York write, "Like the traditional banking system, the shadow banking system conducts credit intermediation. However, unlike the traditional banking system, where credit intermediation is performed 'under one roof'—that of a bank—in the shadow banking system it is performed through a daisy-chain of non-bank financial intermediaries, and through a granular set of steps. These steps essentially amount to the 'vertical slicing' of traditional banks' credit intermediation process…."[20,21] This feature also meant that the precise degree of risk contained in the system became difficult to evaluate and quantify. Thus, when dramatic increases in house prices ceased and defaults in subprime mortgages began to increase, both of which we discuss in more detail in the next section, a great deal of uncertainty about the value of the assets within the system developed.

To sum up, taken together, the optimistic views on the U.S. economy, easy monetary policy, and changes in financial institutions and instruments all contributed to the generation of a bubble in housing prices. Referring back to Figure 5.3, the Case-Shiller Index for the ten large metropolitan areas grew by 125% between January 2000 and April 2006.

This time of rising home prices and economic growth, however, would soon be followed by a series of events that would kick off the U.S. Great Recession, a time of economic difficulty that continued into 2010. The next sections of this chapter trace out the evidence regarding the liquidity-related aspects of this period. As in the previous chapters, our discussion follows the phases that we described earlier. We first note the trigger (1), then changes in the liquidity demanded throughout the economy (2), changes in bank balance sheets (3), changes in bank activity (4), the effect on liquidity and availability of funds throughout the economy (5), and finally, the real effects of the decline in liquidity as observed throughout the economy (6).

5.4 Stage 1: The Trigger

As with our previous two cases, the trigger for the case of the U.S. Great Recession is linked to changes in prices in real estates. For this most recent case, however, the process was a bit more subtle. Here, a flattening out of prices, rather than a steep fall, kicked off the liquidity crisis.

Figure 5.11 provides changes in the Case-Shiller Nationwide Index from the previous quarter. (When the line is above the zero marker, home prices are increasing, whereas when they are below it they are decreasing.) As shown, increases in home prices were strong through the end of 2005. However, prices began to flatten out in 2006, a trend that continued through the first quarter of 2007. We identify this flattening out, together with the information it revealed about the fragility of the market for subprime mortgages, as the trigger for the liquidity crisis that followed.

The key to understanding this link is to take into account the fact that home prices are related to mortgage default rates. To explain, recall our earlier discussion on the easing of lending standards during this period. With this relaxation of standards, people were able to buy homes with mortgages that were a "stretch" financially. In some cases, they planned on selling soon and taking the gain from the increase in price to pay off their mortgage and turn around and buy another house. In other cases, they may have looked to a rise in home prices as an opportunity to refinance and use the newly borrowed money to continue making payments on the home. When home prices flattened out—or even worse, fell—people were left with mortgages that they could no longer afford.

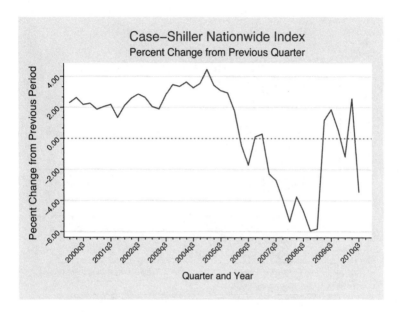

Source: Standard and Poor's

Figure 5.11 *Home prices change from previous quarter*

Indeed, soon after the flattening out in home prices came an increase in delinquency rates on single-family mortgages, as shown in Figure 5.12. (Delinquency rates are for loans and leases still accruing interest and 30 days past due, together with those that are no longer accruing interest.)[22] Delinquency rates on single-family residential mortgages pushed above 2% in the first quarter of 2007, a level that had not been seen since the third quarter of 2002, when the U.S. economy had just emerged from its most recent recession. From that point forward, it marched steadily upward, reaching a level of 11% in the second quarter of 2010. Interestingly, delinquency rates on loans for farmland remained fairly flat through the third quarter of 2008, by which time the broader economic recession was already well entrenched.

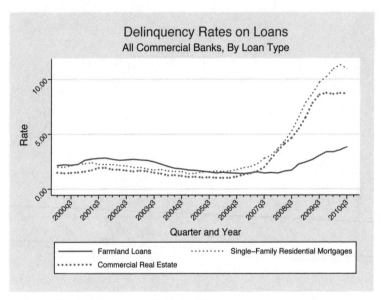

Source: Board of Governors of the Federal Reserve

Figure 5.12 *Delinquency rates*

This flattening out of home prices and increase in default rates was a trigger for the liquidity crisis because of the effect that it had on the value of subprime mortgage-backed securities. Earlier, we discussed the emergence of an alternative financial sector and of Special Purpose Vehicles (SPVs). As we noted, SPVs buy assets, which may be student loans, home mortgages, auto loans, or other types of loans, and then pool them together and issue bonds backed by the assets that they just purchased. (Again, this process is called *securitization*.)[23] They are one way in which banks are able to get assets, such as mortgages, off their balance sheets. One particularly important type of financial instrument that was sold by SPVs was the mortgage-backed security (MBS).[24]

A *mortgage-backed security* is a bond that represents a bundle of mortgages that have been pooled together within the SPV. MBSs played a role in the triggering of the Great Recession because the flattening in home prices and the resulting increase in delinquency rates led to a great deal of uncertainty about the value of mortgage-backed securities.

The idea that default rates are related to home prices is not a new one. Case, Shiller, and Weiss wrote in a 1995 paper "using U.S. foreclosure data by state 1975-93, that periods of high default rates on home mortgages strongly tend to follow real estate price declines or interruptions in real estate price increase." Their analysis controlled for unemployment and income and thus provided an indication of the importance of home prices, over and above changes in these other factors, in affecting default rates. Case, Shiller, and Weiss also refer back to earlier literature that showed the critical role of home prices in determining default rates.

Nevertheless, in 2005, a variety of analysts believed that factors such as interest rates and employment were at least as important as home prices. According to an account of that period at Deutsche Bank, when one analyst found that home prices appeared to be a key determinant of default rates, even after controlling for things such as changes in population and other factors, others were reluctant to accept his conclusions.[25] Thus, when housing prices flattened in 2006 and delinquency rates began to increase in early 2007, concerns about conditions in the housing market and, in particular, in the world of subprime mortgages, heightened.

In February 2007, an announcement by the Federal Home Loan Mortgage Corporation (FHLMC, or more commonly known as "Freddie Mac") said that Freddie Mac would no longer buy the riskiest subprime mortgages and mortgage-related securities.[26,27] This news sent an initial ripple through the system. This was only a ripple, however, as suggested by the response from the Mortgage Bankers'

Association: "Today's announcement by Freddie Mac that it will only purchase subprime mortgages—and mortgage-related securities backed by these subprime loans—that qualify borrowers at the fully-indexed rate will limit the product options and the access to credit for those individuals most in need, many of whom are first time, under-served or minority homebuyers…. The mortgage products that these new standards target are important financial instruments, crucial to helping borrowers get into homes and repair their credit. Regulation that further limits consumer choice is unwarranted."[28]

During the summer of 2007, other problems surfaced. For example, on July 11, rating agency Standard and Poor's announced that it would place on credit watch 612 securities backed by residential mortgages.[29] On August 6, mortgage lender American Home Mortgage filed for Chapter 11 bankruptcy. Its CEO stated, "It is unfortunate that American Home Mortgage, a company which we built into a highly successful business, experienced this sudden reversal of its fortunes due to the unanticipated and rather sudden deteriorations in the secondary and national real estate markets."[30] On August 9, French global bank BNP Paribas froze three funds backed by subprime mortgages,[31] announcing that it was unable to assign values to them: "The complete evaporation of liquidity in certain market segments of the U.S. securitisation market has made it impossible to value certain assets fairly regardless of their quality or credit rating. The situation is such that it is no longer possible to value fairly the underlying U.S. ABS assets in the three above-mentioned funds. We are therefore unable to calculate a reliable net asset value ('NAV') for the funds."[32] A particularly troubling aspect of this event was the fact that it implied a great deal of uncertainty about the value of both these funds and their underlying assets. The problems in the subprime market were reflected in the prices of securities backed by such assets. Early in 2007, an indicator of the value of mortgage-backed securities fell a bit, but then went into virtual free-fall in the second half of the year.[33]

Heightened uncertainty was a key part of the triggering of the liquidity crisis that soon followed. Indeed, Federal Reserve Chairman Ben Bernanke in August 2007 noted, "In contrast, when most loans are securitized and originators have little financial or reputational capital at risk, the danger exists that the originators of loans will be less diligent. In securitization markets, therefore, monitoring the originators and ensuring that they have incentives to make good loans is critical. I have argued elsewhere that, in some cases, the failure of investors to provide adequate oversight of originators and to ensure that originators' incentives were properly aligned was a major cause of the problems that we see today in the subprime mortgage market."[34]

To sum up, this combination of stagnation in housing prices, increases in default rates, and uncertainty in the market for subprime-backed securities were all related to each other and together triggered the crisis in liquidity that soon followed.

5.5 Stage 2: Change in Liquidity Demanded Throughout the Economy

As with the other two episodes that we have considered, the initial trigger led to a shift in liquidity demanded throughout the economy. Broadly speaking, there was an increase in demand for high-liquidity assets and a decline in demand for low liquidity assets. In this section, we describe how this increase was reflected in asset prices and financial markets during this era.

One sign that we look to as indicating a liquidity-crisis-related recession is a decline in the price of assets with low liquidity, such as real estate. We discussed earlier the flattening out of home prices in 2006 and into early 2007. This moderation of 2006 was soon followed by a string of steep declines. Figure 5.11, as previously discussed, provides the indicator for home prices, the Case-Shiller Index, which carefully controls for possible differences across individual homes sold. Figure 5.11 shows changes from the previous quarter for the nationwide index. We see that the declines accelerated in the last half of 2007, posting steep falls through the first quarter of 2009. Figure 5.5, which shows the index itself, indicates the result of these series of declines—average home prices nationwide in 2009 were back down to a level not seen since 2003.

Along with a decline in the price of assets with low liquidity, we would expect to see an increase in the price of assets with very high liquidity. As investors look for the most liquid places to park their funds, they drive up the prices in the markets for high-liquidity assets. Figure 5.13 shows changes in rates on short-term Treasury bills (which move in the opposite direction of prices). The rate on the three-month Treasury bill began to turn down in March 2007, while the four-week turned in April. The months that followed saw steep declines in the four-week, three-month, and six-month bills—a move commensurate with an upswing in the prices of these very liquid instruments.

When we consider the increase in the price of a very liquid asset relative to a less liquid asset, we also see the particularly high premium placed on the most liquid of assets. Figure 5.14 shows the spread between 20- and 1-year U.S. Treasury securities. With the 1-year Treasury being the most highly liquid of these assets, we would expect the most marked decline in its rate with the onset of a liquidity shock, and therefore expect an increase in the spread between the 20-year and the 1-year. (An increase in this spread means that the rate on the 1-year has declined more than the rate on the 20-year; or, alternatively, that the price on the 1-year has risen more than the price on the 20-year.) Indeed, we see an increase in the relative price of the more liquid 1-year security clearly, with the spread rocketing upward in mid-2007.

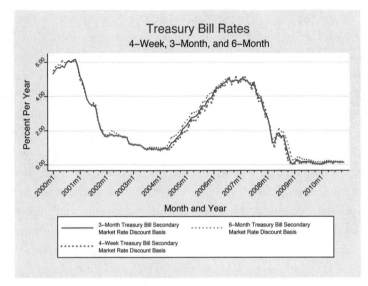

Source: Board of Governors of the Federal Reserve

Figure 5.13 *Liquid assets*

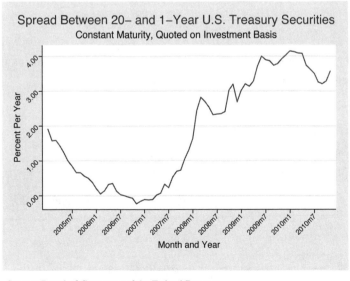

Source: Board of Governors of the Federal Reserve

Figure 5.14 *20-year–1-year spread*

Figure 5.15 shows the spread between the prime rate to the private sector and the rate on short-term government securities. The prime rate to the private sector represents the rate charged to highly rated corporate borrowers, while the rate on short-term government securities is the rate charged to the government. The spread is the difference between the two rates. A higher spread means that private-sector borrowers have to pay more to borrow, relative to the government rate. (It is also equivalent to a decline in the price of a loan to the corporate sector relative to one to the government.) Here, we see a small increase in 2005 and again in 2006, but then a jump in this spread in 2007, just as the problems in the subprime mortgage market were emerging. Since the government instrument is more liquid than the corporate one, this rise is consistent with an increase in the price of the more liquid asset relative to the less liquid asset.

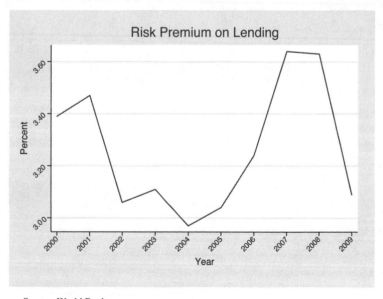

Source: World Bank
Risk premium on lending = prime rate minus Treasury bill rate, %

Figure 5.15   *Risk premium*

To sum up, our most recent example of a liquidity crisis illustrates the classic signs that we set out in Chapters 2 and 3—a fall in the price of illiquid assets, an increase in the price of liquid assets, and an increase in the relative price of liquid to illiquid assets. In the next section, we turn to how these changes in prices in asset markets impacted bank balance sheets, the third phase in the flow-chart shown in Figure 5.1.

5.6 Stage 3: Changes in Bank Balance Sheets

We examine bank balance sheets to see whether the changes that we would expect to occur in a liquidity crisis happened in the case of the U.S. Great Recession. We would expect to see a fall in the value of bank assets with low liquidity, namely loans; bank deposits either falling or changing little; and a decline in bank equity. Thus, we look directly at the main categories of bank balance sheets—assets with low liquidity (loans), liabilities (deposits), and the value of bank equity (capital stock). Interpretation of the data for this case is a bit complicated by the alternative financial system that developed in the preceding years. Thus, some of the changes that we would expect to see at banks may instead show through in the bank alternatives, so we sometimes also bring in other evidence.

For a broad snapshot, Figure 5.16 provides total assets and total liabilities for all commercial banks in the United States. There is a distinct leveling off in both assets and liabilities beginning in April 2008, just after the time of the triggering events discussed in the previous section. As for the breakdown within assets, Figure 5.17 shows data on bank credit from all commercial banks in the United States; the figure also shows information on loans and leases, which are one component of bank credit.[35] Here, we also see a distinct leveling off in bank credit and in loans and leases starting in early 2008.

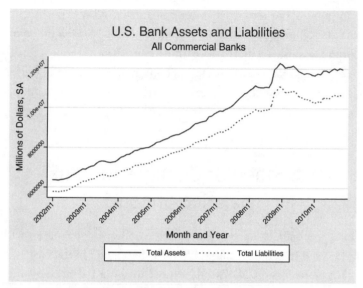

Source: Board of Governors of the Federal Reserve

Figure 5.16 *Total assets and liabilities*

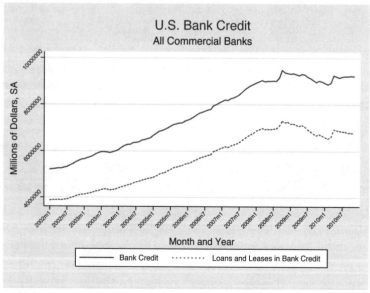

Source: Board of Governors of the Federal Reserve

Figure 5.17 *Bank credit*

Examining the breakdown in types of loans is also of interest. Figure 5.18 shows information on commercial and industrial (C & I) loans, real estate loans, and consumer loans. Real estate loans clearly started to level off in 2008, and the total value of real estate loans shrank during a number of months in mid-2008. Slowing in C & I and consumer loans did not occur until a bit later, a point which we discuss further in the next section. Other assets held by banks are shown in Figure 5.19. Both cash and government securities in bank assets were fairly flat throughout this time period. Thus, these data suggest that the leveling off in bank assets during the time just after the liquidity shock came in the form of stagnation in loans, a change consistent with the framework that we set out for the events of a liquidity crisis.

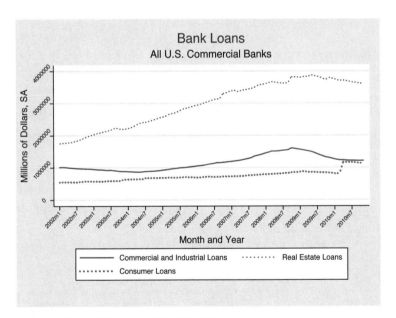

Source: Board of Governors of the Federal Reserve

Figure 5.18 *Breakdown of loans*

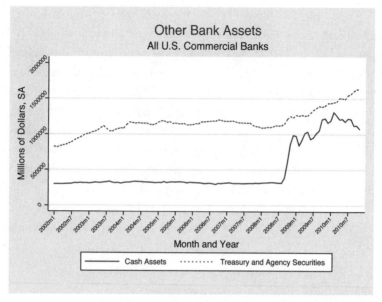

Source: Board of Governors of the Federal Reserve

Figure 5.19 *Other bank assets*

As for the liabilities side of the balance sheet, Figure 5.20 shows deposits at all commercial banks. There is not much change in deposits in 2007 and 2008, as we would have expected. Finally, Figure 5.21 shows total equity capital at FDIC[36]-insured commercial banks, as an indication of the overall banking sector.[37] Here, we see a distinct leveling off in capital after 2007, a move again consistent with our framework for a liquidity crisis.

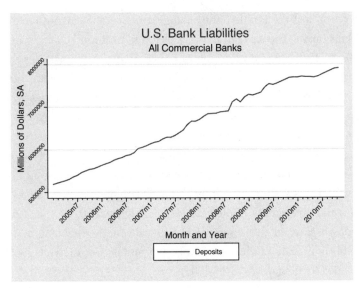

Source: Board of Governors of the Federal Reserve

Figure 5.20 *Bank liabilities*

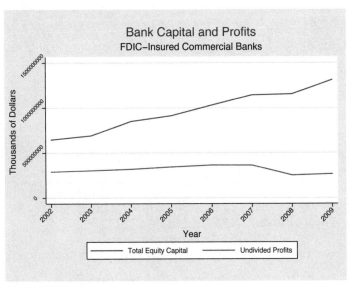

Source: FDIC

Figure 5.21 *Bank capital–FDIC-insured banks*

We noted earlier that the changes in financial institutions and markets during the early to mid-2000s led to profound changes in the nature of financing and the role of banks. Figure 5.22 provides some information on changes occurring in the alternative banking sector that developed during that time. The figure shows liabilities in the alternative banking system (*shadow bank liabilities*) and those in traditional banks. The steep increase in liabilities in the alternative sector, as it expanded in the late 1990s and early 2000s, is clearly shown. However, between the summer of 2007 and the first quarter of 2010, the size of this system shrank by about $5 trillion, which is also clearly shown in the figure.[38] Referring back to Figure 5.10, we can also see the downsizing in the assets within the alternative banking system, with both the value in finance companies and issuers of assets backed securities turning down after 2007.

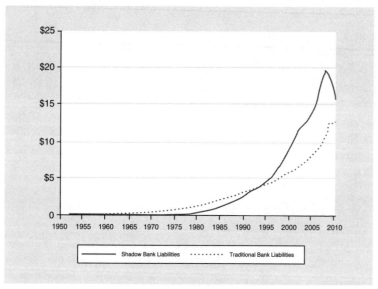

Source: Flow of Funds Accounts of the United States as of 2010:Q1 (FRB) and FRBNY.

Zoltan Pozsar, Tobias Adrian, Adam Ashcraft, and Hayley Boesky. "Shadow Banking." Federal Reserve Bank of New York Staff Reports, no. 458 July 2010.

Figure 5.22 *Alternative banking system*

In earlier chapters, we discussed the problems in the banking sector around the time of a liquidity shock. These problems are clearly evident for the case of the U.S. Great Recession as well. Throughout late 2007 and into 2008, the news was filled with stories of troubles in the banking sector. From write-downs at Citigroup in October 2007, to Bank of America's takeover of Countrywide Financial announced in January 2008, to a bank run at IndyMac, and, perhaps most memorable, the bankruptcy of Lehman in September 2008, signs of severe problems in the U.S. financial system were clear.[39] One piece of data on views of the financial system is provided in Figure 5.23. It shows the spread between AA-rated (i.e., top-quality) financial and nonfinancial commercial paper. The spread is the difference in interest rates that financial and nonfinancial companies must pay. A positive spread means that financial firms must pay more than nonfinancial firms, whereas if the spread is zero, firms in the two sectors are charged the same amount. As the figure shows, this spread was virtually at zero from 2000 until it began to spike up at the end of 2007, which means that financial firms had to pay more for loans than nonfinancial firms; it suggests that financial firms were viewed as relatively riskier and less desirable borrowers in comparison to nonfinancial firms. In October 2008, this spread jumped 63 basis points from the previous month, as the dramatic events in the financial system described previously unfolded.

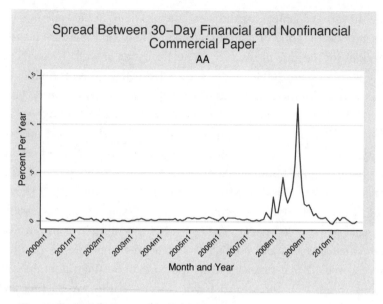

Source: Board of Governors of the Federal Reserve

Figure 5.23 *Financial versus nonfinancial commercial paper*

5.7 Stage 4: Banks Change Activities to Bolster Balance Sheets

Faced with changes in balance sheets such as those discussed earlier, banks must act to shore up their positions. Here, as was the case with Japan, a series of policy actions that took place at the same time complicate our analysis. Particularly important was the dramatic series of policy moves made by the Federal Reserve and the U.S. government more generally to try to assist the U.S. financial sector. Many of these moves followed from the passage in October 2008 of the Emergency

Economic Stabilization Act of 2008.[40] This Act was intended to "immediately provide authority and facilities that the Secretary of the Treasury can use to restore liquidity and stability to the financial system of the United States."[41] Among other things, it established the Troubled Assets Relief Program (TARP), raised the level of deposits insured by the FDIC, and allowed the Federal Reserve to pay interest on balances that banks held at a Federal Reserve Bank. Under the authorization of TARP, the U.S. Treasury Department established the Capital Purchase Program (CPP), also in October 2008, via which it purchased shares of U.S. banks. It distributed $205 billion to 707 financial institutions in that initiative.[42]

Also important during this time period was a series of initiatives by the Federal Reserve aimed at increasing liquidity in financial markets. The Fed created a range of programs that could be used for borrowing from the Fed. As one example, the Asset-Backed Commercial Paper Money Market Mutual Fund Liquidity Facility (AMLF) lent money to banks and bank holding companies that would be used to buy asset-backed commercial paper from money market mutual funds. This facility was set up on September 19, 2008. To give an idea of the magnitude of this one program, between September 22 and the end of September, $159 billion was borrowed by institutions ranging from Bank of New York Mellon to JP Morgan Chase and State Street Bank. These funds were used to purchase asset-backed commercial paper from money market mutual funds such as Dreyfus, Janus, and T. Rowe Price, among others.[43] Other Fed policy initiatives also aimed to increase liquidity in the financial markets, including the Commercial Paper Funding Facility and the Term Asset-Backed Securities Loan Facility.[44] Figure 5.24 provides data on the timing and magnitude of some of these facilities.

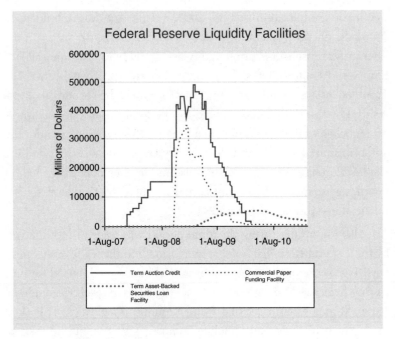

Source: Board of Governors of the Federal Reserve

Figure 5.24   *Fed liquidity facilities*

Taking into account these policy initiatives is particularly important for understanding the behavior of banks in the wake of the liquidity shock. The extraordinary provision of funds to the financial system shows up clearly in the data. Figure 5.19, as introduced earlier in the chapter, shows the jump in cash assets held by banks in the fall of 2008. More broadly, there is an increase in total bank assets, as shown in Figure 5.16. Thus, when examining changes in bank behavior, we must keep in mind these policy actions and their overall effect on bank balance sheets.

As one indicator of changes in bank behavior in the wake of the liquidity shock, we can examine the magnitude of overall bank credit, as well as the provision of various types of loans. As we pointed out earlier, one way in which banks could act to shore up their positions would be to shift away from low liquidity assets, such as loans. Referring back again to Figure 5.17, we see that there is an uptick in bank credit and in loans and leases in the early fall of 2008. This was the time period during which the government was extending a large amount of financial resources to banks. Beginning in November 2008, however, the value of credit on the asset side of bank balance sheets began to shrink. It continued to fall into early 2010. Loans and leases followed the same path.

As for types of loans, Figure 5.18 provides some information. Commercial and industrial loans began to shrink in November 2008, while real estate loans were flat. Loans to consumers were also largely unchanged. Thus, despite the injection of funds into banks, lending did not increase. What did banks do with the funds received? Figure 5.19 provides some indication. It shows the amount of bank assets in cash and in Treasury and Agency securities. (Treasury and Agency securities include, for example, U.S. government Treasury securities.) We see a huge jump in cash in the fall of 2008, which increased even more through the beginning of 2010. The value of bank assets in Treasury and Agency securities also increased steadily after the fall of 2008. Thus, as expected, we observe an increase in bank holdings of very liquid assets.

As a final indicator of the assets side of the balance sheet, Figure 5.25 shows the ratio of banks' highly liquid reserves—cash and deposits with the Central Bank—to their assets that are claims on (i.e., loans to) the private sector and others. If this ratio is high, it suggests that banks are keeping their assets as liquid as possible, rather than lending them out in ways that might reduce their liquidity. (We also showed this indicator for Japan.) We see that it climbed dramatically in 2008, indicating an increased preference for liquidity.

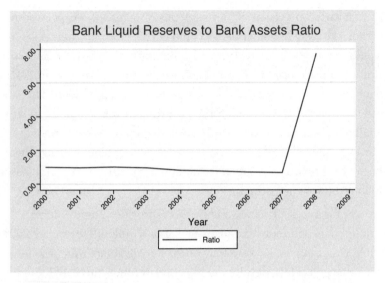

Source: The World Bank
Ratio of bank liquid reserves to bank assets is the ratio of domestic currency holdings and deposits with the monetary authorities to claims on other governments,
nonfinancial public enterprises, the private sector, and other banking institutions.

Figure 5.25 *Reserves to assets ratio*

On the liabilities side of the bank balance sheet, Figure 5.20
shows that deposits increased fairly steadily throughout this period.
Bank capital, as provided for FDIC-insured institutions (refer to
Figure 5.21), increased from 2008 to 2009, reflecting the injection of
capital by the U.S. Treasury Department.

In summary, we have in fact observed the changes that would be
expected in the wake of a liquidity shock. Banks shifted away from low
liquidity assets into assets with very high liquidity. Bank deposits were
fairly steady. Bank capital, boosted by government intervention,
increased a bit. Again, as with the U.S. Great Depression and Japan's
Lost Decade, the classic signs of a liquidity crisis show up in the balance sheets of banks.

5.8 Stage 5: Effect on Liquidity and Availability of Credit Throughout the Economy

Our hypothesis is that changes in bank behavior induced by a liquidity shock in turn impact the availability of funds throughout the economy. Fewer funds become available for assets with low liquidity. In particular, we would expect a decline in availability of credit to individuals and firms within the economy.

As a first indicator, information on credit to consumers is provided in Figure 5.26. Here, we show total credit outstanding to consumers. There is a distinct downturn beginning in November 2008. The chart also shows a breakdown across two types of consumer credit—revolving and nonrevolving. (Neither of the two categories includes loans secured by real estate.) Revolving credit includes things like credit card debt, which are short-term and are paid off soon. Nonrevolving credit includes things like car loans and student loans, which are paid off over a longer period of time. The decline in 2008 stems from a fall in the revolving credit category. This is not surprising, as this is short-term credit that could be reduced quickly.

As for mortgage debt, information on total mortgage debt outstanding is shown in Figure 5.27. Total mortgage debt outstanding rose dramatically through 2007 and then leveled off in 2008, after which it began to fall. This decline came after the time of financial turmoil that we described earlier. We also have data on mortgage debt broken down by type of holder, which is provided in Figure 5.28. The fall-off in total mortgage debt after 2008 is from a decline in the debt held by commercial banks, as well as that held by savings institutions. Taken together, the decline in both mortgage debt and in consumer credit are consistent with our hypothesis of the effect of a liquidity shock on credit in the economy—we observe net tightening of credit to the household sector.

217

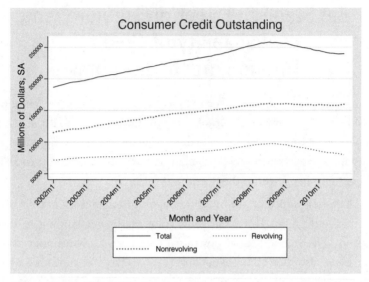

Source: Board of Governors of the Federal Reserve

Figure 5.26 *Credit to consumers*

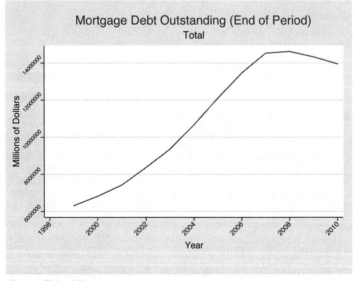

Source: Federal Reserve

Figure 5.27 *Total mortgage debt outstanding*

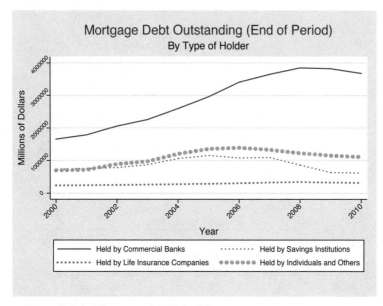

Source: Board of Governors of the Federal Reserve

Figure 5.28 *Mortgage debt outstanding by holder*

Further information on credit availability to households is provided by a senior loan officer survey. Figure 5.29 shows the net percentage of loan officers who said they were tightening standards for consumer credit card loans, other consumer loans, and prime mortgages. Whenever the line is above zero, it means that more are tightening than are not. The data show a steep climb in the share tightening beginning at the end of 2007. Interestingly, although subprime loans were the initial area of problems in real estate, loan officers were tightening standards even for prime mortgages, as well as credit card loans and other consumer loans.

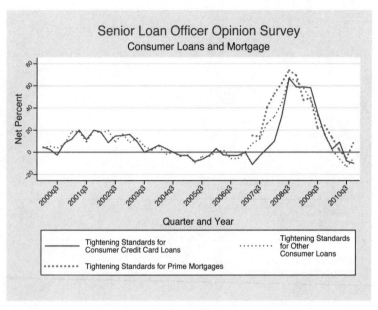

Source: Board of Governors of the Federal Reserve

Figure 5.29 *Loan officer survey—consumers*

As for the corporate sector, we already presented some evidence suggesting a decline in credit to firms. Figure 5.18 showed that lending by commercial banks for commercial and industrial loans fell off after November 2008. For a broad view, Figure 5.30 shows information from U.S. flow of funds data. It shows credit market borrowing by type of borrower, and we provide information for nonfarm, nonfinancial corporate businesses and for nonfarm, nonfinancial, noncorporate businesses. The latter includes businesses other than farms and financial firms that are not incorporated, in other words small businesses in a wide variety of sectors other than finance and farming. The credit market borrowing shown here is a wide category, incorporating things such as corporate bonds, bank loans, and commercial mortgages. Thus, it provides a broad view of the extension of credit to the business sector. As shown in Figure 5.30, there is a dramatic decline in credit market borrowing by both corporate and noncorporate businesses. The decline begins in early 2007 for the corporate sector and a bit later for noncorporate firms.

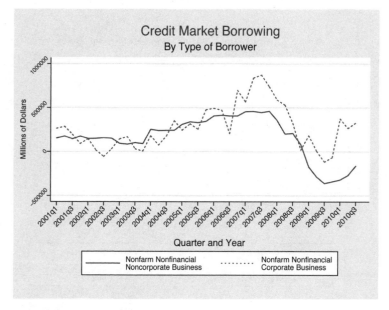

Source: U.S. Flow of Funds

Figure 5.30 *Business credit market borrowing*

Further information on credit availability to firms is again provided by the senior loan officer survey. Figure 5.31 shows the net percentage of respondents to the survey who said they were tightening standards for commercial and industrial loans, as well as the net percentage who said they were increasing the spreads over the costs of funds that they charged to borrowers. Thus, whenever the line is above zero, it means that more are tightening than are not or more are increasing spreads than are not. The information is broken down into responses regarding loans to large and medium firms and responses regarding loans to small firms. Figure 5.31 shows a sizeable increase in both tightening and in spreads for both groups of firms starting in

2007. A greater share reported tightening continuing into 2010. These data suggest that loans were becoming both more difficult to get and more costly for borrowers during this time period.

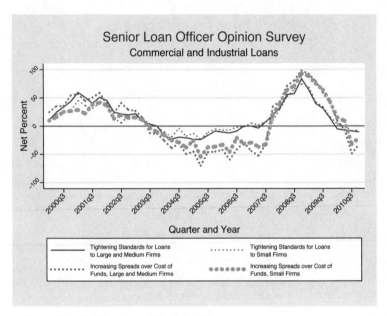

Source: Board of Governors of the Federal Reserve

Figure 5.31 *Loan officer survey—business loans*

The survey also reports on whether senior loan officers are tightening standards on commercial real estate loans, which we show in Figure 5.32. Here, we also see a jump up in the net percent reporting tightening standards, with a full 87% reporting tightening in the fourth quarter of 2008.

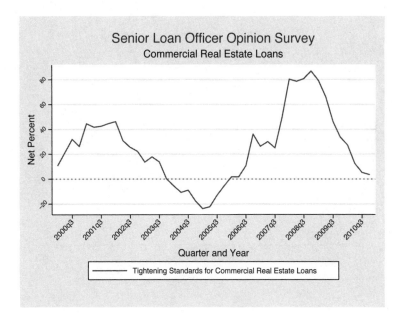

Source: Board of Governors of the Federal Reserve

Figure 5.32 *Loan officer survey–commercial real estate loans*

Finally, as an indicator of overall credit availability we consider total domestic credit to the private sector in Figure 5.33. This should tell us generally how available credit was within the economy. Here, not surprisingly and consistent with the other evidence that we presented, there is a leveling off and then a steep drop-off in domestic credit after 2007.

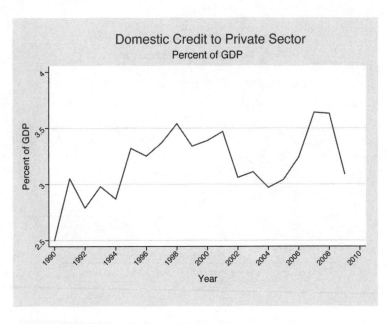

Source: World Bank
Domestic credit to private sector refers to financial resources provided to the private sector, such as through loans, purchases of nonequity securities, trade credits,
and other accounts receivable, that establish a claim for repayment.

Figure 5.33   *Domestic credit to the private sector*

5.9 Stage 6: Real Effects of Decline in Liquidity Observed Throughout the Economy

As the final stage of a liquidity shock, we expect the impact of the
shrinking of credit to be felt throughout the real economy. The shock
moves "from Wall Street to Main Street." To illustrate this stage of the
crisis, we focus especially on real estate and construction—sectors
that generally require credit to function but that need this credit for

assets (building, homes, etc.) with relatively low liquidity—as well as on small businesses, for similar reasons.

Figure 5.34 provides information on new housing starts, which tells us about whether new activity is being undertaken that would have required financing to get started. Figure 5.35 shows data on new building permits issued, which provides similar insights. Both figures show remarkable declines in activity starting in the early months of 2006. A few additional points stand out. First, referring to Figure 5.34, new housing starts did not show a significant decline during the recession that occurred at the beginning of the 2000s. Second, both starts and permits issued remained subdued into the end of 2010; the continued low levels suggest that the construction sector remains depressed.

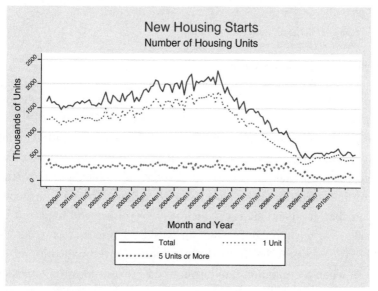

Source: U.S. Census Bureau, http://www.census.gov/const/www/newresconstindex_excel.html
Seasonally adjusted, annual rate

Figure 5.34 *Housing starts*

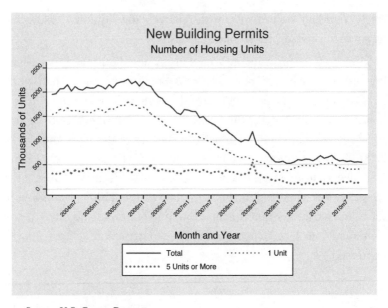

Source: U.S. Census Bureau
Seasonally adjusted, annual rate

Figure 5.35 *New building permits*

As with the U.S. Great Depression and Japan's Lost Decade, we examine trends in prices during this time period. Figure 5.36 shows changes in the Consumer Price Index (CPI) (General and Without Food and Energy) from the previous year. Any changes below the zero line mean that prices are falling (deflation), while those above the zero line mean that prices are rising (inflation). The CPI for goods other than food and energy (which may be volatile and impacted by changes in weather and swings in world oil prices) was generally increasing around 2% from the previous year through the end of 2008, when the inflation rate began to edge closer to zero. (Changes in overall prices reflect the huge swing in oil prices in 2008.) These data show that the United States did not experience the prolonged period of deflation witnessed during the Great Depression or in Japan during the early 2000s. Nevertheless, any increases in the general price level (i.e., inflation) were definitely subdued. As for home prices, earlier we discussed the severe deflation in that sector that occurred during this period and that we showed in Figure 5.11.

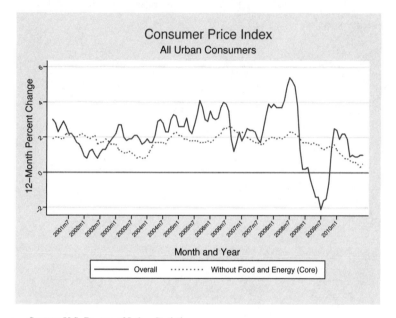

Source: U.S. Bureau of Labor Statistics

Figure 5.36 *Price trends*

As for broad measures of economic activity, Figure 5.6 provides information on changes in Gross Domestic Product (GDP) after the liquidity shock. (GDP is the broadest measure of all the economic activity taking place in a country.) The figure shows that in the wake of the liquidity shock, growth in GDP turned negative beginning in 2008. The huge fiscal stimulus package passed into law in early 2009 boosted growth in the second half of that year, but it bounced back down (but remained positive) in subsequent quarters. The Federal Reserve's Industrial Production Index is another indicator of broad economic activity; it encapsulates production in manufacturing, mining, and utilities and is shown in Figure 5.37. This indicator shows a profound slide from the end of 2007, with a bottoming out in mid-2009. It has recovered since then, as we write this in early 2011, but the level remains below where it was just prior to the onset of the liquidity shock.

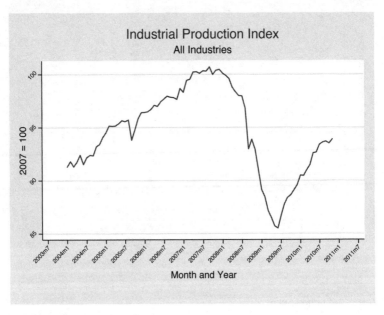

Source: U.S. Bureau of Labor Statistics

Figure 5.37   IP Index

Information on employment conditions in the United States also provides information about aggregate economic activity and whether the shock to liquidity reverberated beyond the financial sector. Figure 5.38 provides the most commonly cited statistic, the unemployment rate, which marks the proportion of those who are actively seeking and available for work who are not able to find jobs, as a percent of the total labor force. Figure 5.38 shows the onset of economic distress dramatically. The rate began to increase in 2007 and reached a high of 10.1% in October 2009. It dropped down a bit in subsequent months, but remained substantially above the pre-downturn level through the end of 2010. Figure 5.38 shows another indicator that provides information about the state of employment that may not be captured by the headline unemployment rate. It shows the number of people who are working part-time because they are not able to find full-time jobs. This number also climbed during the most recent economic downturn in the United States, suggesting that some portion of those who were employed were not able to find as much work as they would have liked to.

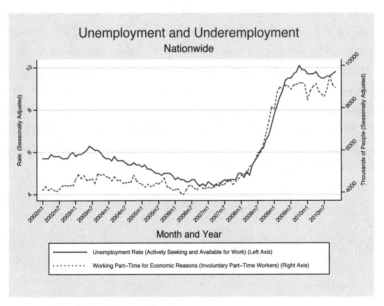

Source: U.S. Bureau of Labor Statistics

Figure 5.38 *Unemployment and underemployment*

For more insight on employment, the top panel of Figure 5.39 shows numbers on job openings rates and job hiring rates. The rate of openings, which is the number of openings divided by the sum of employment and job openings, plummeted in the private sector beginning in mid-2007. The public sector picked up some of the slack on occasion, but public and private sector openings remained below their pre-downturn levels at the end of 2010. The bottom panel of Figure 5.39 shows job hires. These data show a similar pattern: a downturn in opportunities in the private sector, with occasional increases in job hires in the public sector. One point to note here is that the federal government initiated a large fiscal stimulus program in 2009; however, state and local governments, which are also included in the government total, have been cutting back.

As our final indicators of the employment situation, Figure 5.40 provides numbers for the long-term unemployed and discouraged workers. The long-term unemployed have been out of work for at least 27 weeks, and their numbers climbed beginning in 2008. Discouraged workers are those who are not even trying to find jobs because they have given up hope that any jobs are available. Here, also, we see a huge increase starting in 2008. Both of these trends suggest that the U.S. Great Recession has had severe and long-lasting effects on those unable to find work.

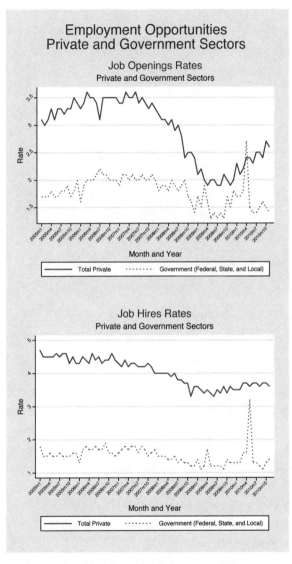

Source: U.S. Bureau of Labor Statistics JOLTS Database
The job openings rate is the number of openings divided by (employment plus job openings).
The hires rate is the number of hires as a percent of total employment.

Figure 5.39   *Employment opportunities*

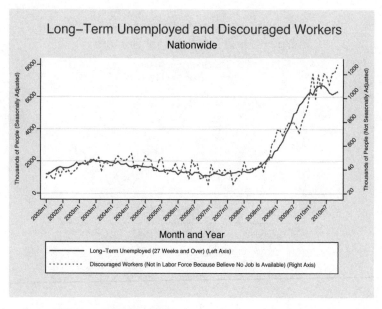

Source: U.S. Bureau of Labor Statistics

Figure 5.40 *Long-term unemployed and discouraged workers*

We have suggested that liquidity crises are characterized by an inability to get credit for things such as creating or expanding businesses, which would feed through to real effects and show up in things such as aggregate economic activity and opportunities for employment. The evidence that we have presented on unemployment, underemployment, job openings, and long-term unemployed and discouraged workers is consistent with that story. Additional evidence of this aspect of a liquidity crisis is provided from the results of a survey of small businesses. Small businesses are traditionally more reliant on bank loans than are large ones, since they do not have the access to equity and bond markets that large corporations do. Furthermore, loans to small businesses are an illiquid asset—they cannot easily be sold to another party in a timely fashion at a predictable price. Thus, this sector may be a likely place to see the possible impact of a shock to the availability of funds.

A 2008 survey of small and mid-sized businesses provides some insight as to the problems that faced this sector. Of course, survey results are based on the perceptions of respondents, but the outcome of the survey provides some indication of conditions in the small business sector. As shown in Figure 5.41, more than one-third of the smallest businesses were unable to get adequate financing in 2007 and 2008. For slightly larger businesses, about a quarter were unable to get the funding they felt they needed. Figure 5.42 provides additional information about this sector. It shows that small businesses used bank loans substantially less for financing after the onset of the liquidity crisis. (Alternative sources may have included things such as personal savings, business savings, or personal or business credit cards.)

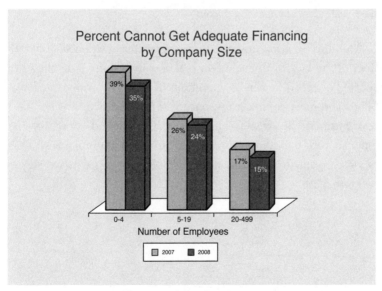

Source: National Small Business Association 2008 Survey of Small and Mid-Sized Businesses, available at http://www.nsba.biz/docs/2008bizsurvey.pdf.

Figure 5.41   *Small business financing*

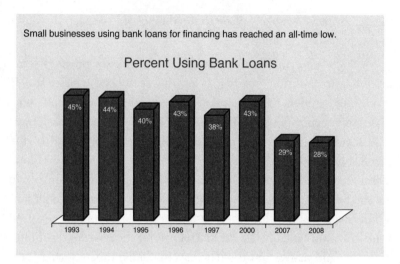

Source: National Small Business Association 2008 Survey of Small and Mid-Sized Businesses, available at http://www.nsba.biz/docs/2008bizsurvey.pdf.

Figure 5.42 *Small business bank loans*

The survey also provides some suggestive evidence about the effect of the lack of financing on real activity. Figure 5.43 shows the reported effects on business operations of problems with capital availability. The most common response was that the firm was unable to grow business or expand operations. The second most common response was that the company had to reduce employees. These responses resonate with the lackluster job openings data we showed in Figure 5.39.

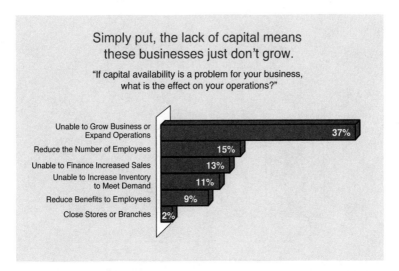

Source: National Small Business Association 2008 Survey of Small and Mid-Sized Businesses. Survey conducted in February 2008. Available at http://www.nsba.biz/docs/2008bizsurvey.pdf.

Figure 5.43 *Effects of lack of capital*

As a final piece of information about conditions for small businesses, Figure 5.44 shows more recent data on ability to secure enough financing. Problems with obtaining funds actually worsened throughout 2008 and continued through July 2010. Thus, despite the fact that overall economic growth had picked up by that time, the small business sector continued to face a relatively difficult financing situation.

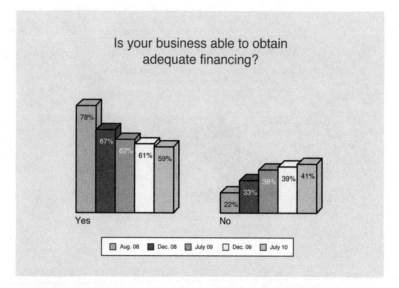

Source: National Small Business Association 2010 Mid-Year Economic Report.
Available at http://www.nsba.biz/docs/nsba_2010_mid-year_economic_report.pdf.

Figure 5.44 *Recent financing for small businesses*

All these measures—declining activity in housing, declining prices, sluggish aggregate growth, and persistent and high unemployment—taken together provide a good idea of the overall level of economic activity in the United States after the impact of this most recent liquidity shock. The information on conditions for small businesses at that time provides further supportive evidence. Although there was apparently some recovery according to certain statistics, evidence also exists that some of these problems persisted through at least late 2010.

5.10 Conclusion

As with Chapters 3 and 4 on the Great Depression in the United States and Japan's Lost Decade, the evidence presented in this chapter has illustrated how a liquidity shock may be transmitted throughout the economy, as the banking sector shifts away from its traditional function of channeling funds from depositors to borrowers. The credit tightening in turn impacts the real sector and overall economic activity.

The case of the United States Great Recession is distinct in at least two ways. First, the monumental changes in financial institutions, instruments, and markets played a role perhaps even more profound than in our previous two cases. Second, the resolution of this episode remains unknown. Indeed, in 2010, a full three years after the initial stages of the liquidity shock, unemployment remained high, small businesses reported difficulties obtaining loans, growth in credit remained subdued, and housing prices were still far below their peak levels. The U.S. government exercised the levers of both monetary and fiscal policy, to unprecedented degrees. Yet, the aftershock of the liquidity crisis persisted. Our concluding chapter provides some thoughts as to what policy may be able to do to both mitigate the impact of liquidity shocks and to recover quickly when they do occur.

Endnotes

1. For more details on how this period may be viewed as related to a liquidity shock, please see Chacko, George and Evans, Carolyn L. 2011. "A Liquidity-Shock Perspective on The U.S. Great Recession." Working Paper.

2. In the direct feedback mechanism, bank sales of assets with very low liquidity lead to further declines in the prices of those assets. In addition, there is propagation to other markets throughout the economy. With the dramatic drop in prices in the market for assets with very low liquidity, banks turn to selling somewhat more liquid assets, which leads to drops in prices in these other markets. Rounds of selling move through a wide range of markets, as banks shift from market to market searching for ways in which to take the least losses on their sales.

3. As noted in Chapter 3, the yield is essentially the rate of return that investors receive by buying a particular instrument. It moves in the opposite direction of the price of the asset. If an investor is willing to accept a low yield on an asset, it means that she intrinsically values that asset more than another asset with a higher yield. An increase in the yield is equivalent to a decline in its price, while a decrease in the yield is like a rise in its price.

4. Nathalie Girouard, Mike Kennedy, Paul van den Noord, and Christophe Andre (2006) "Recent House Price Developments: The Role of Fundamentals." Organization for Economic Cooperation and Development (OECD). Economics Department Working Papers, No. 475, p. 22.

5. Joint Center for Housing Studies (2004) "Hot Housing Market Masks Eroding Affordability and Mounting Risks." Press release from http://www.jchs.harvard.edu/media/son_release_2005.html, June 13, 2004.

6. White House Press Release (2005) "President Meets with Economic Team." http://georgewbush-whitehouse.archives.gov/news/releases/2005/08/20050809-3.html, August 9, 2005.

7. International Monetary Fund (IMF) (2006) "United States: Staff Report for the 2006 Article IV Consultation." IMF Country Report No. 06/279, http://www.imf.org/external/pubs/ft/scr/2006/cr06279.pdf.

8. Federal Reserve Release "Press Release." March 20, 2001. http://www.federalreserve.gov/boarddocs/press/general/2001/20010320/.

9. For some discussion, see J. John Taylor (2008) "The Financial Crisis and the Policy Responses: An Empirical Analysis of What Went Wrong." Bank of Canada Festschrift in Honour of David Dodge, November 2008.

10. For some discussion, see J. John Taylor. (2008) "The Financial Crisis and the Policy Responses: An Empirical Analysis of What Went Wrong." Bank of Canada Festschrift in Honour of David Dodge, November 2008.

11. As we noted in Chapter 2, regulations on capital adequacy requirements state that banks are required to hold a certain amount of equity capital that depends on the riskiness of the investments that it makes.

12. One might argue that bank executives, like all business managers, make decisions based primarily on economic realities rather than accounting results. However, everything that we have stated on an accounting basis also holds on an economic basis. For example, banks target a certain level of capital relative to equity on an economic basis.

13. Others have referred to this set of institutions as the "shadow banking system."

14. The economic incentives to maintain an adequate level of capital would remain, no matter the regulatory framework.

15. A number of excellent and extensive pieces have been written describing this alternative banking system. For example, see Zoltan Pozsar, Tobias Adrian, Adam Ashcraft, and Hayley Boesky (2010) "Shadow Banking." Federal Reserve Bank of New York Staff Reports, no. 458 July 2010; and Gary Gorton and Andrew Metrick (2010) "Regulating the Shadow Banking System." Fall 2010 conference of the Brookings Papers on Economic Activity (BPEA).

16. Gregory Zuckerman (2009) *The Greatest Trade Ever: The Behind-the-Scenes Story of How John Paulson Defied Wall Street and Made Financial History*. New York: Crown Business.

17. Ivy L. Zelman, Dennis McGill, Justin Speer, and Alan Ratner (2007) "Mortgage Liquidity du Jour: Underestimated No More." Credit Suisse, March 13, 2007, p. 24.

18. Ivy L. Zelman, Dennis McGill, Justin Speer, and Alan Ratner (2007) "Mortgage Liquidity du Jour: Underestimated No More." Credit Suisse, March 13, 2007, p. 12.

19. Andrew Tilton (2007) "The Subprime Slump and the Housing Market." U.S. Economics Analyst, Goldman Sachs, February 23, 2007, pp. 4-6.

20. Zoltan Pozsar, Tobias Adrian, Adam Ashcraft, and Hayley Boesky (2010) "Shadow Banking." Federal Reserve Bank of New York Staff Reports, no. 458 July 2010.

21. What we call the alternative banking system has been called the *shadow banking system* by a number of researchers, including the authors of this paper (Zoltan Pozsar, Tobias Adrian, Adam Ashcraft, and Hayley Boesky (2010) "Shadow Banking." Federal Reserve Bank of New York Staff Reports, no. 458 July 2010).

22. Federal Reserve Statistical Release "Charge-Off and Delinquency Rates on Loans and Leases at Commercial Banks." http://www.federalreserve.gov/releases/chargeoff/default.htm.

23. A number of excellent and extensive pieces have been written describing this alternative banking system. For example, see Zoltan Pozsar, Tobias Adrian, Adam Ashcraft, and Hayley Boesky (2010) "Shadow Banking." Federal Reserve Bank of New York Staff Reports, no. 458 July 2010; and Gary Gorton and Andrew Metrick (2010) "Regulating the Shadow Banking System." Fall 2010 conference of the Brookings Papers on Economic Activity (BPEA).

24. Basel Committee on Banking Supervision. The Joint Forum, Bank for International Settlements. Report on Special Purpose Entities, September 2009.

25. Gregory Zuckerman (2009) *The Greatest Trade Ever: The Behind-the-Scenes Story of How John Paulson Defied Wall Street and Made Financial History*. New York: Crown Business.

26. Federal Reserve Bank of St. Louis "The Financial Crisis: A Timeline of Events and Policy Actions." http://timeline.stlouisfed.org/index.cfm?p=timeline#, accessed February 22, 2010.

27. In its 2006 Annual Report, Freddie Mac notes, "We announced on February 27, 2007 that we would implement stricter investment standards for certain subprime ARMs with short adjustment periods originated after September 1, 2007. First, we will only buy ARMs, and mortgage-related securities backed by those loans, for which borrowers have been qualified at

the fully-indexed and fully-amortizing rate in order to help protect these borrowers from the payment shock that could occur when the interest rates on their ARMs increase. Second, we will limit the use of low-documentation underwriting for these types of mortgages to help ensure that borrowers have the income necessary to afford their homes." Report available at http://www.freddiemac.com/investors/ar/pdf/2006annualrpt.pdf.

28. Mortgage Bankers Association "MBA Questions Freddie Mac's New Underwriting Standards for Subprime Lending." Press Release, February 27, 2007. http://www.mortgagebankers.org/NewsandMedia/PressCenter/ 48715.htm, accessed February 22, 2010.

29. Standard & Poor's. Primary Credit Analysts: Susan E Barnes, Robert B Pollsen, Ernestine Warner; Secondary Credit Analysts: Michael Stock, Monica Perelmuter, Martin Kennedy; Global Practice Leader-ABS/RMBS Ratings: Rosario Buendia; Chief Quality Officer-SF Ratings: Thomas G Gillis. "S&PCORRECT: 612 U.S. Subprime RMBS Classes Put On Watch Neg; Methodology Revisions Announced." Standard & Poor's Ratings Direct, July 11, 2007. http://www2.standardandpoors.com/spf/pdf/fixedincome/SubprimeRevision0710.pdf.

30. http://www.sec.gov/Archives/edgar/data/1256536/000091412107001892/ am9746838-99_1.txt.

31. "American Home Mortgage Investment Corp. Files for Chapter 11 Bankruptcy." Press release, August 6, 2007. http://www.ny.frb.org/research/global_economy/Crisis_Timeline.pdf.

32. "ABS" refers to Asset Backed Securities. BNP Paribas "BNP Paribas Investment Partners temporarily suspends the calculation of the Net Asset Value of the following funds: Parvest Dynamic ABS, BNP Paribas ABS EURIBOR and BNP Paribas ABS EONIA." Press release, August 9, 2007. http://www.bnpparibas.com/en/news/press-releases.asp?Code=LPOI-75W9PV&Key=BNP%20Paribas%20Investment%20Partners%20temporaly%20suspends%20the%20calculation%20of%20the%20Net%20Asset%20Value%20of%20the%20following%20funds%20:%20Parvest%20Dynamic%20ABS,%20BNP, accessed February 22, 2010.

33. We refer to the ABX.HE index. See Gary Gorton (2008) "The Panic of 2007," in *Maintaining Stability in a Changing Financial System*,

Proceedings of the 2008 Jackson Hole Conference, Federal Reserve Bank of Kansas City, 2008 for discussion.

34. Federal Reserve Chairman Ben Bernanke's remarks, "Housing, Housing Finance, and Monetary Policy," at the Federal Reserve Bank of Kansas City's Economic Symposium, Jackson Hole, Wyoming, August 31, 2007.

35. The other big component is securities, such as Treasury and agency securities. See http://federalreserve.gov/releases/h8/current/default.htm for more information.

36 The Federal Deposit Insurance Corporation (FDIC) is a government corporation that provides deposit insurance, guaranteeing the safety of deposits in the banks that are members of FDIC.

37. This group of FDIC-insured banks does not include all banks that are in the other figures on all U.S. commercial banks. However, it does include all of the most important banks in the United States. We were unable to locate data on equity capital at all U.S. commercial banks.

38. Zoltan Pozsar, Tobias Adrian, Adam Ashcraft, and Hayley Boesky (2010) "Shadow Banking." Federal Reserve Bank of New York Staff Reports, no. 458 July 2010.

39. Very useful timelines of this time period are provided by the Federal Reserve Bank of Saint Louis (http://timeline.stlouisfed.org/index.cfm?p=home) and the Federal Reserve Bank of New York (http://www.ny.frb.org/research/global_economy/policyresponses.html).

40. H.R. 1424 was the vehicle for the "Emergency Economic Stabilization Act of 2008." See http://thomas.loc.gov/cgi-bin/bdquery/z?d110:HR01424:@@@L&summ2=m&. Also see http://www.gpo.gov/fdsys/pkg/PLAW-110publ343/html/PLAW-110publ343.htm.

41. This text is taken from Public Law No: 110-343, which contains the provisions put forward in the Emergency Economic Stabilization Act of 2008. The Public Law itself is available from http://www.gpo.gov/fdsys/pkg/PLAW-110publ343/html/PLAW-110publ343.htm.

42. U.S. Department of the Treasury "Investment Programs, Capital Purchase Program." http://www.treasury.gov/initiatives/financial-stability/investment-programs/cpp/Pages/capitalpurchaseprogram.aspx.

43. The Federal Reserve provides this information. See http://www.federalreserve.gov/newsevents/reform_amlf.htm.

44. Information about the range of programs is available at http://www.federalreserve.gov/monetarypolicy/bst_reports.htm.

References

Adrian, Tobias and Hyun Song Shin. 2009. "The Shadow Banking System: Implications for Financial Regulation." Federal Reserve Bank of New York Staff Reports, no. 382 July 2009.

Adrian, Tobias and Hyun Song Shin. Forthcoming. "Liquidity and Leverage." *Journal of Financial Intermediation*.

Adrian, Tobias and Hyun Song Shin. 2009. "The Shadow Banking System: Implications for Financial Regulation." Federal Reserve Bank of New York Staff Reports, no. 382 July 2009.

Adrian, Tobias and Hyun Song Shin. 2008 "Liquidity and Leverage." Federal Reserve Bank of New York Staff Reports, no. 328. May 2008; revised December 2010.

Basel Committee on Banking Supervision. The Joint Forum, Bank for International Settlements, Report on Special Purpose Entities, September 2009.

Bernanke, Ben. 2007. "Housing, Housing Finance, and Monetary Policy." Remarks at the Federal Reserve Bank of Kansas City's Economic Symposium, Jackson Hole, Wyoming, August 31, 2007.

Bhardwaj, Geetesh and Rajdeep Sengupta. 2008B. "Where's the Smoking Gun? A Study of Underwriting Standards for U.S. Subprime Mortgages." Federal Reserve Bank of St. Louis, working paper.

Brunnermeier, Markus K. 2009. "Deciphering the Liquidity and Credit Crunch 2007-2008." *Journal of Economic Perspectives*, Volume 23, Number 1. Winter 2009. pp. 77-100.

Case, Karl E., Robert J. Shiller, and Allan N. Weiss. 1995. "Mortgage Default Risk and Real-Estate Prices: The Use of Index-Based Futures and Options in Real Estate." National Bureau of Economic Research Working Paper No. 5078.

Chacko, George and Evans, Carolyn L. 2011. "A Liquidity-Shock Perspective on The U.S. Great Recession," working paper.

Demyanyk, Yuliya and Otton Van Hemert. 2007. "Understanding the Subprime Mortgage Crisis." (December 10) Stern School of Business, New York University, working paper.

Demyanyk, Yuliya. 2009. "Ten Myths about Subprime Mortgages." Federal Reserve Bank of Cleveland Economic Commentary. http://www.clevelandfed.org/research/commentary/2009/0509.cfm.

DiMartino, Danielle and John V. Duca. 2007. "The Rise and Fall of Subprime Mortgages." *Economic Letter—Insights from the Federal Reserve Bank of Dallas*. Vol. 2, No. 11, November 2007.

Girouard, Nathalie, Mike Kennedy, Paul van den Noord and Christophe Andre. 2006. "Recent House Price Developments: The Role of Fundamentals." Organization for Economic Cooperation and Development (OECD). Economics Department Working Papers, No. 475. http://www.oecd.org/officialdocuments/displaydocument-pdf?cote=ECO/WKP(2006)3&doclanguage=en, January 2006.

Gorton, Gary. 2008. "The Panic of 2007." In Maintaining Stability in a Changing Financial System, Proceedings of the 2008 Jackson Hole Conference, Federal Reserve Bank of Kansas City, 2008.

Gorton, Gary. 2009. "Slapped in the Face by the Invisible Hand: Banking and the Panic of 2007." Federal Reserve Bank of Atlanta Jekyll Island Conference Proceedings.

Gorton, Gary and Andrew Metrick. 2010."Regulating the Shadow Banking System." Fall 2010 conference of the Brookings Papers on Economic Activity (BPEA).

Gorton, Gary B. and Nicholas S. Souleles. 2005. "Special Purpose Vehicles and Securitization" FRB Philadelphia Working Paper No. 05-21. September 1, 2005. Available at SSRN: http://ssrn.com/abstract=713782 or doi:10.2139/ssrn.713782.

Greenlaw, David, Jan Hatzius, Anil Kashyap, and Hyun Song Shin. 2008. "Leveraged Losses: Lessons from the Mortgage Market Meltdown, U.S. Monetary Policy Forum Report No. 2." http://research.chicagogsb.edu/igm/events/docs/USMPF-final.pdf.

International Monetary Fund (IMF). 2006. United States: Staff Report for the 2006 Article IV Consultation, IMF Country Report No. 06/279, http://www.imf.org/external/pubs/ft/scr/2006/cr06279.pdf.

Pozsar, Zoltan, Tobias Adrian, Adam Ashcraft, and Hayley Boesky. 2010. "Shadow Banking." Federal Reserve Bank of New York Staff Reports, no. 458 July 2010.

Shiller, Robert. 2007. "Understanding Recent Trends in House Prices and Homeownership." Kansas City Federal Reserve Bank, Jackson Hole Conference Proceedings.

Taylor, John. 2008. "The Financial Crisis and the Policy Responses: An Empirical Analysis of What Went Wrong." Bank of Canada Festschrift in Honour of David Dodge, November 2008.

Tilton, Andrew. 2007. "The Subprime Slump and the Housing Market." U.S. Economics Analyst, Goldman Sachs, February 23, 2007, pp. 4-6.

Zelman, Ivy L., Dennis McGill, Justin Speer, and Alan Ratner. 2007. "Mortgage Liquidity du Jour: Underestimated No More." Credit Suisse. March 13, 2007.

Zuckerman, Gregory. 2009. *The Greatest Trade Ever: The Behind-the-Scenes Story of How John Paulson Defied Wall Street and Made Financial History*. New York: Crown Business.

---

chapter 6

Conclusion

In the previous chapters we described a phenomenon—liquidity risk and liquidity shocks—whose effects work primarily through financial institutions. As a result, economic contractions that occur due to liquidity crises behave differently than standard recessions.

An obvious question that comes to mind is whether there are ways to lessen the effects of liquidity shocks. If a liquidity shock occurs in the financial markets, can public policy be used to mitigate its effects on financial markets and institutions as well as shield the nonfinancial sector of the economy? In this chapter, we deal briefly with this question as we conclude the book.

6.1 A Liquidity Crisis

A liquidity shock starts when there is a drop in the fundamental value of securities in a market—for example, mortgage prices. This is usually caused by an economic event of some type, such as in increase in loan defaults. This economic event leads to substantial net selling in a particular market or set of markets as well as an increase in volatility. The selling and volatility increase results in a large drop in prices. This price drop then feeds back and causes further illiquidity in that market and further drops in prices. In the case of the Great Recession in the United States for example, the initial liquidity shock occurred in the market for mortgage-backed securities (MBSs) and its derivatives such as collateralized mortgage obligations (CMOs) and credit default swaps (CDSs) on MBSs.

The initial liquidity shock is then transmitted to other markets by financial institutions. This transmission occurs because those banks[1] that are holding securities in the market initially affected by the liquidity shock suffer losses on their securities holdings. These losses in turn deplete their equity capital. As their capital decreases, the banks become too highly leveraged and therefore are forced to sell assets to reduce their debt to equity ratio.[2] The assets they sell are not those in which they have taken losses because this market is already suffering a liquidity problem, which would only be exacerbated if additional selling were attempted. Instead, these banks sell assets in other markets. If a large enough group of banks is affected by the initial shock and the selling then becomes systematic, that is, a large number of banks are forced to sell similar assets, then a liquidity shock develops in these other markets as well. Thus, the liquidity shock is transmitted to these other markets. The process then keeps repeating, and the initial liquidity shock is transmitted to multiple markets. This process is known as financial contagion and results in a macro liquidity crisis.

Finally, the liquidity shock gets transmitted to the nonfinancial sector of the economy because the banks and other financial institutions that have had their capital reduced cannot conduct normal lending and other credit provision operations.[3] The lack of sufficient capital prevents them from taking additional risk on their balance sheets, and therefore they slow down or stop lending, especially to riskier borrowers. This results in a credit crisis, or *credit crunch*, in the nonfinancial sector of the economy, which in turn causes a contraction in the overall economy. Thus, the original liquidity shock has been transmitted to the real sector of the economy.

They key to understanding how a liquidity shock spreads is the transmission process that occurs via the normal responses of banks to changes in their balance sheets and funding availability. Therefore the key to mitigating the effects of a liquidity shock is to prevent this transmission process from occurring.

6.2 Bank Accounting Changes

A critical step in the transmission mechanism is the need on the part of banks to liquidate assets because they have just faced a sudden reduction of their capital. Therefore one obvious idea to prevent this liquidation is to simply allow them to not recognize losses, which are the source of the capital reduction. In other words, change the accounting rules so that losses in market value do not have to be immediately recognized by banks on the balance sheets. If these losses are not recognized, a bank's capital will not be reduced. This was tried in the United States at the start of the Great Recession, for example, when the bank accounting rules were changed in 2009. This was also done in Japan in 1997 during its protracted recession.

However, the problem with this approach is the fact that bank executives, like all business managers, make decisions based primarily on economic realities rather than accounting results. So, while accounting rules may delay the recognition of the reduction in a bank's accounting or regulatory capital, its economic capital has nevertheless decreased. All the steps leading to the transmission of liquidity shocks are based on economic, or market, values (including the changes to the market value balance sheets of banks). Therefore, while the accounting or regulatory rule changes might reduce the pressure a little bit to liquidate assets, a bank will still need to sell assets as its short-term debtholders start calling in their debt or refuse to roll it over. The reduction in economic capital will similarly force banks into decreasing lending.

What an accounting rule change like this does is create so-called *zombie-banks*—banks that are in reality troubled, or even dead, but they are still seemingly healthy by accounting standards. This is precisely what occurred in Japan due to its accounting rules, which allowed banks to delay recognizing bad loans. In the end, this accounting rule did nothing to curb the reduction in credit in the economy, and the Japanese government finally forced a number of these banks into default when they changed the accounting rule back to a market value basis in 1999. Thus, changes in accounting rules and other information merely to alter the perception of what is occurring in a bank or in a market do not generally work—business managers and investors make decisions based on what is really happening in markets; that is, based on market values, and it is difficult to fool them by simply changing the accounting rules.

6.3 Bank Nationalization

This brings us back to the question of how to effectively prevent the transmission of a liquidity shock from occurring. The transmission process takes place because banks experience a reduction in their equity capital. Therefore, the most direct way to prevent the banks' capital from being reduced (on a market value basis) is to somehow increase their equity capital through another channel. One obvious way to do this is for banks to issue equity. The issuance of equity directly increases a bank's capital by increasing shareholder equity. If enough equity can be issued by a bank, the increase in its capital can be enough to offset the decrease in its capital from a liquidity shock. In this case, the bank would not feel any pressure to quickly liquidate assets or reduce its provisioning of credit.

The problem, of course, is that few investors are willing to step in during a liquidity shock and buy bank equity, particularly in large quantities as is often needed. Furthermore, banks are reluctant to try to issue equity during a shock because a signal would then go out to the markets that their balance sheet has been substantially negatively affected. This signal might cause a panic and a subsequent run on the bank, which would only exacerbate the liquidation pressure they face.[4]

Rather than issuing equity to investors, a solution is to issue equity to a governmental agency, such as the U.S. Treasury or the U.S. central bank (the Federal Reserve); or to issue equity to some type of sovereign fund, such as the U.S. Social Security Trust Fund. To solve the problem of banks' unwillingness to issue equity (due to the negative signal it sends to the financial markets), the equity issue can be mandatory. This is precisely what the country of Sweden did when the real estate market there imploded and it underwent a liquidity shock in 1991-1992. The government took equity stakes in most of the banks in the country. Soon afterward, the liquidity crisis ended and confidence returned to the Swedish financial system. The U.S. government did the same thing during the Great Recession of 2008-2009. Soon after the global investment bank Lehman Brothers failed, the U.S. forced the most important U.S. financial institutions to issue warrants (a type of equity) to the government. The institutions that were forced to participate in this plan included such major banks as Citibank, J.P. Morgan, Bank of America, and Goldman Sachs. Once this plan was put in place, all bank runs ceased and confidence returned to U.S. financial institutions. Similarly during the Savings & Loan crisis of the late 1980s and early 1990s in the United States, the government effectively took equity stakes in most of the savings and loan associations in the United States and stopped a liquidity crisis from ballooning into a major economic crisis.

Either a partial or complete bank nationalization—the purchase of bank equity by a government—can thus be an especially effective way of dealing with a liquidity crisis. However it is important to ensure that the bank returns to the hands of private investors after the liquidity crisis is over by giving the bank the ability to call back or repurchase the equity it issued to the government.

6.4 Debt Guarantees

Having the national government guarantee bank deposits and other short-term bank debt is often discussed as an alternative to dealing with troubled banks. In the case of a liquidity crisis, guaranteeing bank deposits may be able to slow down the transmission of a liquidity shock. One of the reasons a bank is forced to liquidate assets is that its short-term debtholders call in (force repayment of) their debt or they refuse to roll over their debt. The debtholders are worried that the bank may experience large enough losses from the liquidity shock to deplete all of the bank's capital and drive the bank into default. Having a government guarantee short-term bank debt alleviates this bank run problem because it eliminates the possibility of short-term debtholders losing money on the bank debt they own, thus obviating the need for short-term debtholders to call in their loans.

However, the crux of the problem—reduced bank capital—is not solved by simply guaranteeing the bank's short-term debt. As a result the bank eventually needs to liquidate assets to reduce its overall leverage. It will also need to reduce its lending activities because it does not have enough capital to support its previous levels of lending. So, even though the liquidity crisis is averted in the short term, it may continue to slowly propagate around the financial system, and the original liquidity shock's effects on the nonfinancial sector will not be averted, only delayed.

Furthermore, if bank shareholders know that a policy exists of guaranteeing bank deposits when a liquidity crisis starts, it makes it more likely that banks will take more risk without being assessed a higher cost of capital by bondholders. This leads to the classic moral hazard problem where liquidity shocks are more likely to occur because banks lend to riskier sectors, which have a higher likelihood of precipitating liquidity crises.

Finally, a liquidity crisis is one where many banks systematically find themselves in trouble. If a government guarantees all of these banks' debts, the government may find itself overleveraged and in risk of defaulting on its obligations. This is one of the important reasons why countries such as Iceland and Ireland got into trouble during the Great Recession; and why other countries such as Spain had serious difficulty issuing bonds, as potential investors were concerned that the country was on the verge of guaranteeing the debt of all the banks in the country.

6.5 Central Bank Lending

Rather than averting a bank run by guaranteeing short-term bank debt, a somewhat more effective way to deal with the problem of liquidity shock transmission is to replace the existing short-term debtholders (who are making a run on the bank). This can be done by having a central bank serve as a lender of last resort and provide short-term loans to banks. Thus, rather than becoming an equity holder of banks through a bank recapitalization, the government (through the central bank) becomes a short-term bondholder of these banks. The banks are free to use the loans provided by the central bank to pay off their other short-term debts, which allows the bank to stop a bank run. Therefore, the central bank replaces the existing short-term bondholders who are calling back their loans to the bank.

Direct central bank lending can be an effective strategy in delaying the transmission of liquidity shocks because by averting a bank run it decreases the pressure on banks to sell assets. It is the selling of assets, after all, that allows the original liquidity shock to get transmitted into other markets.

The Panic of 1907 in the United States was a classic example of how a lender of last resort averted a financial system meltdown as a result of a major liquidity crisis. The liquidity crisis started with the bankruptcy of a brokerage house, Gloss & Kleeberg. As a result of actual and feared loan losses to this brokerage house, a bank run started and spread to all the major banks in New York. The liquidity crisis became so bad that the New York Stock Exchange nearly collapsed. A U.S. central bank did not exist at the time. Therefore, to mitigate the liquidity crisis, the financier J.P. Morgan used a large amount of his own money and convinced other bankers to do the same to loan money to banks that were facing bank runs. Thus, J.P. Morgan and the other bankers together acted as a de facto central lender of last resort. As a result of this experience, the U.S. Congress passed a law a few years later officially establishing a U.S. central bank, known as the Federal Reserve Bank.

While direct central bank lending to banks delays the need for banks to sell assets, it does not solve the issue of bank capital reduction. If markets that are experiencing a liquidity shock do not have any changes in the fundamental value of their securities, this approach works fine because the banks' capital has only been reduced temporarily.[5] However, if the liquidity shock is induced by a reduction in the fundamental value of securities (such as a reduction in real estate values—the most common fundamental value reduction leading to liquidity shocks), bank capital likely gets reduced permanently. In this case, direct central bank lending to banks does not solve the capital reduction problem—it simply delays the inevitable liquidation of assets and reduction in credit provision. This is why even though J.P. Morgan and his fellow bankers were able to prevent a financial system collapse during the Panic of 1907, they were not able to prevent the transmission of this liquidity shock into the nonfinancial sector. Due to the bank panic, from mid-1907 thru 1908 the U.S. economy experienced a substantial contraction, with industrial production dropping 11% and unemployment increasing from 3% to 8%. The economy eventually rebounded when the banks had built their equity capital back up and restored previous levels of credit activity.

6.6 Monetary Policy

Perhaps the most widely used approach to mitigate liquidity shocks (as well as most other financial or economic crises) is for the central bank of a country to flood the financial markets with liquidity; that is, increase money supply. This, for example, entails the central bank going into the government bond markets and purchasing bonds. The purchase of bonds puts money into the hands of investors (the sellers of the bonds), who can then put this money to work by making loans and thereby inducing more economic activity, as well as providing liquidity into those markets suffering liquidity crises. Whenever any kind of crisis starts, central banks around the world start injecting large amounts of additional liquidity into the financial markets. During the Great Recession, the U.S. central bank injected more than $2 trillion into the financial system. Other central banks, from Europe to Asia followed suit.

However, in the case of a liquidity shock, injecting liquidity into the markets is not very effective. It does not solve the underlying problems. In theory, the additional liquidity being provided by a central bank to government bondholders should quickly work its way into those markets that are experiencing the liquidity shock(s) because these markets offer the highest risk premium (due to the extra liquidity risk premium from the shock). However a market experiencing a liquidity shock has also become substantially more volatile, that is, risky. Thus, bondholders are reluctant to invest the additional liquidity into this market. Instead they put their money into banks in the form of deposits or into short-term government bonds and other ultra high quality debt. As a result, banks are flooded with liquidity and short-term interest rates drop in financial markets.

We saw precisely this phenomenon occur during the Great Recession and other smaller liquidity crises such as the U.S. Savings & Loan crisis and the Long Term Capital Management crisis of 1998.

As an example, however, during the Great Recession neither retail nor institutional investors quickly directed the central bank's cash into those markets experiencing liquidity problems or into investments that might stimulate economic activity. Investors instead directed the extra cash into banks, which then directed the cash into reserve deposits with the central bank. Thus, the extra liquidity created by the central bank showed up right back on the central bank's balance sheet. Essentially, what the central bank had done was to increase the supply of money on both the left- and right-hand sides of its balance sheet, which was doomed to be ineffective.[6]

A much more effective way for liquidity injections to work is if the central bank, rather than buying government bonds, directly purchases assets or securities in those markets experiencing the liquidity shock—a policy known informally as *quantitative easing*. For example, during the Great Recession the U.S. central bank started directly purchasing mortgage-backed securities, corporate bonds, and other nontraditional securities whose markets were experiencing severe liquidity problems. By stepping in to these markets and acting as buyers, the central bank was doing what most investors and dealers were reluctant to do—acting as a counterparty to sellers in these markets. In effect, the central bank had become the "dealer of last resort" (in addition to its normal job of being the lender of last resort) and provided liquidity to sellers in these markets, thus directly reducing the liquidity problems that some of these markets were experiencing.

6.7 Fiscal Spending

Another effective, but difficult, approach is to use fiscal spending measures. Basically, incremental government spending can be used to alleviate the effects of a liquidity shock, but because government spending is an inefficient way to solve liquidity-related issues, it takes a lot of extra spending to have a meaningful effect. The extra government spending generates additional cash flow for individuals and businesses. By doing this, government spending replaces the cash that bank credit would have provided to individuals and businesses. Thus, it directly helps to alleviate the effects of liquidity shocks—a lack of credit availability—to the nonfinancial sector of the economy. The additional government spending can also indirectly help alleviate the effects of liquidity shocks on financial institutions and can improve the ability of individuals and businesses to make interest and principal payments on any debt they may have. If a liquidity shock's effects on banks stem from loans they are holding—such as defaults on business loans or mortgages—the improved ability of borrowers to repay their loans increases the values of these loans. The increase in value in turn improves banks' capital, thus alleviating the pressure to liquidate assets (and further transmitting a liquidity shock) and reduce credit.

During the late 1930s and early 1940s, massive fiscal spending by the United States on building up its armed forces for World War II pulled the United States out of its economic problems stemming from the Great Depression. Similarly, in Japan massive fiscal spending at the start of its decade-long contraction helped start pulling Japan out of its economic downturn.

However, the problem with using fiscal policy is that it often does not take place soon enough or in a sufficiently large enough quantity. In the case of the Great Depression in the U.S., the U.S. government tried increasing government spending years before the spending for World War II occurred. However, this expansion in government spending was largely offset by increases in taxes so that the net increase in spending was fairly small relative to the decrease in GDP.[7] So, it took a long time to generate the political will for huge deficit spending. In Japan, while the government moved fairly quickly to increase deficit spending, the political will to maintain this level of spending quickly died,[8] and therefore so did the initial positive effects of the spending on Japan's economy.

6.8 Preventing Liquidity Crises

Perhaps the most effective way to deal with a liquidity crisis is simply to put in place policies to prevent them from happening. Examples of such policies could be restricting the ability to sell securities to a certain window of time during the day or restricting short-selling—thus possibly preventing security values from decreasing much and a liquidity shock from ever starting. Another example would be to have stringent bank regulation in place to prevent banks from becoming very big. The resulting fragmented banking system could possibly prevent a liquidity shock from getting transmitted due to the lower likelihood of banks having the same securities on the LHS of their balance sheets. This lower correlation among bank investment portfolios results in a lower likelihood of a systematic asset liquidation,[9] which is the key ingredient necessary for the transmission of liquidity shocks.

The problem with these types of approaches is that while they may prevent liquidity crises and therefore economic downturns, they may also limit economic growth. For example, additional rules on equity markets may increase the cost of equity capital for all firms. Additional regulation on banks may increase the cost of debt capital for all firms as banks passed on the additional regulatory costs[10] to borrowers.

Finally and possibly most importantly, financial markets and institutions, like most businesses, are innovative. If the costs due to a policy are high enough that it curtails certain activities that they would like to do, they will innovate their way around them. That was precisely the genesis of the securitization phenomenon as banks tried to get around bank capital regulations.

So, in the end, it may be the case that liquidity crises go hand-in-hand with an efficiently functioning economic system. The liquidity crises might simply be a normal byproduct of, for example, behavioral phenomena on the part of investors, so that trying to indirectly offset investor behavior patterns with policies and regulations directed at other parts of the financial system simply makes the global economic system less efficient.

Endnotes

1. From this point on, we use the term *bank* generically to represent financial institutions of all types that perform asset liability management (investment banks, commercial banks, insurance companies, funds, etc.).

2. This pressure is coming from one of two sources. First, with this much leverage, a bank cannot conduct normal investment operations such as lending because its risk capital is too low. Therefore, to get back to normal operations it needs to sell assets and use this cash to pay down debt. The other pressure comes from holders of its short-term debt. These holders, recognizing the bank's increased probability of default, will likely call in their debt. This again puts pressure on the bank to raise cash, and its only means of doing so is by selling assets.

3. One might think that the financial institutions could solve this problem simply by raising their capital levels through equity issuances. However, when financial institutions have suffered a substantial reduction in capital due to losses, it is usually difficult for them to issue equity.

4. This is also likely the reason why investors are reluctant to purchase equity from banks immediately after a liquidity shock. Investors know that only banks that were in serious and immediate danger of default would be willing to risk having a negative signal go out to the markets and thereby risk a bank run.

5. Once the liquidity shock has been mitigated, the fundamental values of the securities held by the bank return back to pre-crisis levels—levels at which banks do not have any losses and therefore nor do they have capital reductions.

6. However, one positive effect of this policy was that while banks were paying depositors very little on their deposits, they were being paid a substantially higher interest rate by the central bank (due to a recent change in policy by the central banks to pay interest on reserve deposits). Thus, the banks

earned an easy, riskless profit from this business, and this profit in turn bolstered their equity capital. As a result, the central bank through somewhat arcane channels managed to directly increase bank capital, perhaps the most effective move it made during the whole Great Recession.

7. For example, the Revenue Act of 1932 pushed up income tax rates for all individuals, especially on lower- and middle-income groups. The corporate tax rate and estate tax rates were increased during this period as well. Furthermore, new taxes such as the Social Security tax and excise taxes were introduced.

8. The main reason for this was the worry about whether the country would be able to pay off all the debt it was quickly incurring due to the huge quantity of the government's spending program.

9. That is, many banks selling the same securities simultaneously.

10. Such as the opportunity costs of not taking full advantage of scale efficiencies or not building sufficient brand equity.

Index

W-X

Y

Z

FINANCIAL TIMES

In an increasingly competitive world, it is quality
of thinking that gives an edge—an idea that opens new
doors, a technique that solves a problem, or an insight
that simply helps make sense of it all.

We work with leading authors in the various arenas
of business and finance to bring cutting-edge thinking
and best-learning practices to a global market.

It is our goal to create world-class print publications
and electronic products that give readers
knowledge and understanding that can then be
applied, whether studying or at work.

To find out more about our business
products, you can visit us at www.ftpress.com.